Searching for Healing

FROM THE NEW AGE

JULIE MELLOR

Copyright © 2013, 2014 by Julie Mellor

All scripture quotations, unless otherwise indicated, are taken from the Holy Bible, New International Version®. NIV®. Copyright © 1973, 1987, 1984 by International Bible Society. Used by permission of Zondervan. All rights reserved.

The website addresses recommended throughout this book are offered as a resource to you. These websites are not intended in any way to be or imply an endorsement by Julie Mellor, nor do I vouch for their content for the life of this book.

All rights reserved. No part of this publication may be reproduced, stored in a retrieval system, or transmitted in any form or by any means – electronic, mechanical, photocopy, recording or any other – except for brief quotations in printed reviews, without the prior permission of the copyright owners.

This book contains advice and information relating to health and medicine. It is designed for your personal knowledge and to help you be a more informed consumer of medical and alternative health services. It is not intended to be exhaustive or to replace medical advice from your physician and should be used to supplement rather than replace regular care by your physician. Readers are encouraged to consult their physicians with specific questions and concerns.

Julie Mellor can be contacted through John Mellor Ministries, www.johnmellor.org

Book design by Jo Edgar-Baker.

Photograph taken by John Mellor at Shakespeare's house, Stratford-upon-Avon.

Printed in Australia.

ISBN: 978-0-646-90918-9

DEDICATION

With deep gratitude, I dedicate my testimony to encouraging everyone who supports the work of Gideons International. Thank you for the part you played in my salvation.

I am sending you to them to open their eyes and turn them from darkness to light, and from the power of Satan to God, so that they may receive forgiveness of sins and a place among those who are sanctified by faith in Me.

Act 26:17

My Testimony

PURPOSE OF THIS BOOK

For most of my life I was a devout atheist. I was aggressively closed to believing in God, until a series of traumatic events brought me to a point where I experienced so much torment and despair that I thought my life was irrevocably ruined and no longer worth living. In desperation, and as a last resort, I challenged God: 'If you're real, please help me!' My cry was answered.

I write my testimony with several readers and purposes in mind. Firstly, I hope this book falls into the hands of people who currently don't have a relationship with Jesus Christ, but are open to learning about how Jesus can transform and heal lives - as He did mine. I also hope to encourage readers who already know Jesus, to be bolder in sharing their own testimonies and the love and power of Christ with people around them, so that everyone knows what is required to spend eternity in heaven, for the Lord 'does not want anyone to perish.' (2 Peter 3:9 ISV)

Part of my testimony discusses my fruitless search for healing through the New Age. In reflecting on my journey, I point out the spiritual risks that come with involvement in the New Age and its false gods. I also list many practices and 'treatments' offered even by medical doctors, chiropractors, fitness instructors and masseurs that are actually of the New Age and therefore pose open doors to demonic influences and oppression. An increasing number of people, mature Christians included, are unwittingly exposing themselves to the demonic realm in their search for health and healing.

Having now devoted my life to serving Jesus through the

healing ministry I share with my husband, John Mellor, I see daily the havoc demonic forces cause in the minds, emotions and bodies of people who are suffering. At the same time, I am privileged to see the evidence of Jesus' reality and power manifest before me each week as I witness hundreds of people being set free from every condition you can name. No condition is too big, hard or impossible for God to heal or solve, which is what you would expect of a loving God who created everything, isn't it?

MY LIFE BEFORE ENCOUNTERING JESUS

I grew up in a relatively normal, stable home in Melbourne. Though life wasn't perfect, I was never abused or mistreated and I never went without anything I needed or wanted. I have always been cheerful and confident, though I was prone to worry. I was fairly popular at school, though I had my share of disappointments and schoolyard betrayals. At school, I was an all rounder and experienced success academically, in sports and also in creative arts. I went on to university and achieved three degrees from Melbourne University and won a scholarship to study for my Master's degree at Cambridge University. As a child and adult, I travelled extensively overseas. Life seemed pretty good. I became a high school English teacher and taught in the private system for 16 years, and I also became Head of Department for 9 years in a large, three-campus school.

Although I had several long term boyfriends, my intention was to never marry. But while I didn't want to marry, I did want to be in a long term monogamous relationship. I had developed a cynical attitude towards men and marriage and wanted to be able to get out of a relationship quickly if things turned boring or unpleasant. I knew that Christians believed that it was a sin to have sex before marriage, so this was one blockage to me thinking I could ever be a Christian.

My upbringing was almost spiritually bereft. I was not taken to church on Sundays or given religious instruction. My only brushes with church were at Easter when I occasionally went along with my Russian Orthodox grandmother to church at midnight for Easter Mass. I thought these services were beautiful because the church was candle lit, there were bright murals on a domed roof, a choir sang from a balcony and the scent of burning frankincense filled the room.

None of my primary school friends were church goers and it was only in the first year of university that I became aware that some friends from high school were Christians or had quietly become Christians at some point. One time they invited me to come along to an event at a 'cafe' near uni - which turned out to be in a church, and the event a Christian youth meeting. While people sat around chatting, every now and then someone would grab the microphone and holler things like, 'Guess what? Jesus loves you!' I silently fumed at my friends. Although these friends tried a few times to invite me along to events, which I suspected were largely attended by Christians, they never openly witnessed to me about Jesus.

Having been approached by students from the Christian Union many times at university when I was sitting on my own, I came to view Christians as fanatics and pests. I also interpreted their approach to me when I was alone to mean that they were a group of odd bods who gathered other loners and strange folk into their group. I was therefore rejecting the idea that I was a loner or odd. When I saw them coming, I would hold up my hand to signal them to stop and called out, 'No thanks, I'm not interested.' I also decided that anyone who believed in 'God' must have had a screw loose in their thinking to have faith in such fairy tales. I concluded that they must have chosen to believe in God and heaven to ease their fear of death.

My parents didn't seem to have any interest in religion when I was growing up. Mum would sigh audibly and roll her eyes at expressions of Christian fervour on television, and my father - a large, imposing man - would be sent to the door to scare away pesky Jehovah's Witnesses. I suppose I picked up on my parents' indifference (perhaps even disdain) for religion, and I adopted this attitude too.

In primary school, when religious instruction was offered, a letter was sent home to inform our parents. I asked my mum to write a letter excusing me from the class, so that I could participate in another activity that I assumed would be more fun and where all of the 'cool' kids would be. My mother wrote the letter without question. I was surprised to discover that I was the only child from my whole year level not attending religious instruction, and I just sat, bored, in another classroom reading a book.

However, when I was 17, my father suddenly started going to church. Having been raised in a nominal Catholic home, he viewed the imminent and unplanned birth of my brother, Lucien, to be a miracle. Lucien's arrival was certainly a great blessing which brought enormous joy to the family, but we thought Dad was losing the plot. However, we did appreciate having an hour of peace and quiet on Sunday mornings while Dad was at church. We mercilessly teased him, pointing out his flaws and hypocrisy and taunted him with jibes such as, 'Oh, that's fine behaviour for a Christian' on the frequent occasions when we riled him to anger. My father's conversion was and is genuine and ongoing, but Dad never witnessed to us about Jesus, so his conversion didn't have much impact on me spiritually.

When I was studying at Cambridge University, I regularly walked through college chapels and visited many of the historic churches around Britain. I have long been a fan of choir music and so attended concerts and evensong at King's College and St John's College – whose choirs are regarded amongst the best in the world. On a number of occasions, tears welled in my eyes at these concerts. At the time, I thought I responded this way because I was surrounded by so much beauty – especially at evensong. Evensong is evening prayer, held around dusk in Anglican churches. In Cambridge college chapels at dusk, the sinking sun shines through the stained glass windows - creating a kaleidoscope of coloured light on the walls. Candles are lit, the architecture is breathtaking and the choirs sound angelic. It's astonishing to reflect now how blind I was to realising that I was actually sitting through a service praising and worshipping God and that what moved me to tears and tugged on my chest was the Holy Spirit. I thought I was just attending a free concert!

A few years after my time at Cambridge, when I travelled through Italy, I spent a good deal of time wandering through churches, both world famous ones and intimate, simple ones in the middle of nowhere. While staying in the Tuscan village of Cortona, I went inside many of its 32 churches and daydreamed about one day moving to Tuscany. I observed the villagers attending mass at the various churches and how they chatted and laughed with their friends as they came out of the church. I envied their close community and sense of belonging. I recall thinking, 'I wish I believed in God.' I decided that my unbelief wouldn't stop me from attending church when I did eventually move to Tuscany: attending church would be the fastest way to make friends and fit in.

It was only a little while after returning from Italy that my life was tipped upside down.

When things went wrong

A series of traumatising incidents and accidents occurred in my life, which led me to make a number of panicked and ill-considered decisions which made my situation worse. In Christian spiritual terms, this was a trap laid by the devil to wreck my life and I fell in headfirst. I had suffered mental, emotional and physical damage and trauma.

I found myself in a state of shock, struggling to accept what had happened to me. My mind was tormented with the thought that my life was ruined beyond repair, and I was over-whelmed with feelings of shame, regret and disbelief. As a result, I suffered crippling anxiety and panic attacks. I had no appetite and when I could force myself to eat, I had no sense of taste or smell, and the adrenaline running through my body sent food straight through my system. I felt burning nausea from my throat to my stomach. My throat was tight and con-stricted and I had trouble swallowing. I hyperventilated and my body shook from nervous tension. I only got one or two hours of fitful sleep each night and the only way I could get to sleep was to play choir music the whole night. This went on for about nine months and I became increasingly exhausted and lost a lot of weight.

During this time, I was still teaching and running an Eng-lish Department. The energy that it took to perform all of the tasks expected of me and to try to appear normal in front of my students and colleagues was enormous. I would often have to dash from my classroom into my office just to shake and hyperventilate from the stress I was under and then try to pull myself together and return to class.

Over this period, I became agoraphobic and dreaded being around people, yet at the same time found it comforting to be around them because their normal routines soothed me. I saw very little of my friends and family over this time and forced myself to have cheery, normal sounding conversations on the phone. All the while I wished time could be reversed and my life could return to the way it had been.

I did try to speak with a close friend and also a doctor about what had happened to me, but they dismissed my experience as nothing major and couldn't see that I had a problem.

Almost delirious from torment and exhaustion, I started contemplating ways of taking my life so I could end the suffering. I wanted my death to seem like an accident for the sake of my family.

While in the midst of this suicidal preoccupation, I received a phone call informing me that Stephen, an ex-boyfriend from years ago, had committed suicide. This news naturally came as a great shock and upset, all the more because I was planning to do the same thing. Stephen had developed a serious mental illness, and clearly the torment of the voices in his head had become too much to bear.

Hope restored

Soon after the shocking news of Stephen's suicide, I seemed to snap back into my right mind and stopped thinking about ending my life. My thoughts took a more positive turn and I made the decision to try to find a way out of my hopeless situation. Somehow I got the idea in my head that there were miracles out there, and I was determined to do whatever it took to get one. I knew no one who had received what I considered to be a miracle - although there were people I knew, including my father, who credited God with acting in their lives. My paternal grandmother had been a heavy smoker and had many miscarriages before my father was born. His birth was credited as a miracle. However, I dismissed this as the eventual natural outcome of my grandmother having given up smoking and resting as much as possible once she became pregnant.

Anyhow, I held onto a glimmer of hope and became focused on searching for a miracle.

Searching for a miracle through the New Age

The only place I knew to start searching for a healing miracle was the New Age. At the time, I don't think I was even too aware that what I was looking into was called 'New Age'. Of course, I had heard the term before, but I didn't realise the full breadth of what fell under the New Age umbrella. Instead, I thought I was looking into alternative health and complementary medicine options.

Having always been a clean-living, health-conscious person, I was often in health food shops where there were free copies of brightly coloured magazines to take. I had taken these magazines on many occasions to flip through articles about vitamins and exercise, and had noted the different types of healing treatments advertised, but I had never had any need to try them. This time, I took the magazines home to study them for possible solutions to my problems.

Within the New Age, there is an endless array of therapies or 'modalities' of healing on offer. Every month sees new combinations and renamed variations of older modalities advertised, which claim to be the latest, most powerful therapy available because the inventor has discovered some special key or long-lost ancient knowledge of the universe that makes all the difference. Looking through the magazines, there were many therapies on offer that I dismissed from the outset as too whacky to be taken seriously - things such as tarot readings, angel guide readings, clairvoyance, crystal healing, re-birthing and past life therapy, all of which seemed ridiculous to me. Instead, I focused mostly on the modalities that presented themselves as scientifically verified.

There are many healing modalities that are marketed as being scientific therapies dressed up to appeal to New Agers. The number of New Age therapies purporting to be based on clinical science is rapidly growing, but the studies they present to support their practice invariably lack scientific rigour and validity. I was never interested in science at school, so like a lot of people, I have limited understanding of scientific theories and my ignorance made me vulnerable to believing the pseudoscience peddled by the New Age. Quantum Physics and its principles are heavily bandied about in these modalities. But who understands Quantum Physics?

Core beliefs underpinning the New Age

New Age practices and goals originate from or are similar to Eastern philosophies and religions, particularly Hinduism, Buddhism and Taoism. Common names used for the New Age concept of God include: Creator, Universal Energy, Divine Energy, Mother Earth, Life Force, Infinite Intelligence and Source. Most people within the New Age believe in a god or higher power, but it isn't the God of the Bible. Their idea of God is of an impersonal force or being that can be harnessed and used for personal benefit. The ultimate aim of people within these spiritual practices is to achieve 'enlightenment', 'higher consciousness' 'god realisation' or 'self-realisation.' They are on a journey to free their souls from the shackles of their body to 'become one with the universe.' In achieving this, they hope to receive the realisation that they are divine in nature, and therefore, God. As God, they can create their own reality and therefore what they believe in is their 'truth', which can be immensely different from another person's reality. The temptation and goals of the New Age are like those Satan used to deceive Adam and Eve in the Garden of Eden when tempted to eat the forbidden fruit:

For God knows that when you eat from it your eyes will be opened, and you will be like God, knowing good and evil. (Genesis 3:5)

New Age followers use practices such as yoga, meditation and vegetarianism in this journey to help discipline the body and free the soul from the confines of the physical world.

The New Age is broadly appealing as there are no rules or morals and there is no concept of sin, guilt or shame, except for what a person chooses as their own moral boundaries. In contrast, Christianity, from the outside, seems to be about rules and restrictions. It's difficult to see Christian principles as principles for freedom when you are spiritually blind and haven't received a revelation from God or read the Bible. One of the most notable revelations for me when I became a Christian was seeing Christian principles from a completely different perspective – from God's perspective - and what as an atheist had seemed like draconian rules were clearly revealed as principles for freedom and right living.

The New Age search is an endless one. Hindus and Buddhists believe in reincarnation and believe it can take many lifetimes to achieve a state of nirvana – the highest state of being or enlightenment. The search is endless because they are not dealing with truth and they are not dealing with the only source of eternal life and pure healing - Jesus:

I am the way and the truth and the life. No one comes to the Father except through me. (John 14:6)

As well as going on a journey in search of higher consciousness, most people involved in the New Age are on a search for truth, peace and healing. Many also become involved in practising some form of therapy because it's an easy way to step into a new, alternative lifestyle and career with no qualifications. Tomorrow you could rent a shop, paint it purple, light candles and incense, dangle some crystals, play rainforest music, invent a name for your therapy, say nice reassuring things to a customer, promise them the world, wave your hand over them for half an hour, charge $100, and voila, you're in business!

Most people who practise New Age therapies offer about half a dozen modalities. This in itself is evidence that no one modality has power to do what is claimed, and even combined together they have no real power. However, as many forms of New Age practices call on a god, energy or presence, that is not Jesus, they are opening a door to the demonic and in most cases they are doing so without realising it.

The New Age is part of the occult, but the work of the devil is more subtly in action. Most New Age practitioners are deceived in believing they are working with the same God and source of light, power and truth as Christians, believing that many roads lead to God. The New Age even has its own teachings on who Jesus is - an ascended master, a prophet or one of many gods; however, it is not Jesus of the Bible. People who are fully immersed in occult practices are aware that they are working with demonic forces and openly worship Satan. However, in the New Age, the practitioners are generally blind to the demonic:

And no wonder, for Satan himself masquerades as an angel of light. It is not surprising, then, if his servants also masquerade as servants of righteousness. Their end will be what their actions deserve. (2 Corinthians 11:14-15)

As I selected the healing modalities I was going to try, I thought I was being wise and clever in choosing the ones that were apparently supported by science. I researched each modality I was considering, making phone calls to ask questions of the practitioners, as well as searching the Internet and ordering books.

NEW AGE HEALING MODALITIES

Just before I recount my experiences of some of the many New Age modalities I tried, I must emphasise that I am in no way promoting any form of New Age healing or practice: quite the opposite. I detail my experiences to give readers a little understanding of some of the available therapies which people around the world, including Christians, are being drawn to try. Now, as a deep-end Christian, I have understanding of the dangers involved in dabbling with the New Age practices I tried. If we are to seek God for healing, it must only be through Jesus. To understand who Jesus is and what we can claim in His name, we must read the Bible for ourselves. The Bible is perfectly clear that we should not seek out or worship false gods, spirits, the dead, angels, images, statues, fortune tellers, astrology, etc:

> *Let no one be found among you who sacrifices their son or daughter in the fire, who practices divination or sorcery, interprets omens, engages in witchcraft, or casts spells, or who is a medium or spiritist or who consults the dead. Anyone who does these things is detestable to the LORD; because of these same detestable practices the LORD your God will drive out those nations before you.* (Deuteronomy 18:10-12)

> *Ignorant are those who carry about idols of wood, who pray to gods that cannot save.* (Isaiah 45:20)

It is worth pointing out that in many forms of New Age healing, there is often one aspect of truth mixed in amongst the false beliefs. Warping truth is one of the main ways the devil works in our lives to create confusion and havoc, just as he did in the Garden of Eden where Satan deceived Adam and Eve into believing that God was withholding good things from them. It is often this germ of truth which is the hook to convince people that everything else about the practice is acceptable. Also, it is common to find that people who are the founders, discoverers and developers of a mode of New Age healing are charismatic and successful in some field, and so people look to them almost as gurus or mentors who have chartered a path to where they themselves want to go.

You might wonder where the harm is in some of the practices I tried and will soon discuss. The danger is in the core beliefs behind the practices, which in the New Age are linked, even though the practitioner may not be aware, to either Eastern religions or Spiritualism. Whenever a force, energy, source or false god is called upon or credited with being the source of healing or power – a force that is not the Holy Spirit of God accessed through the name of Jesus Christ of the Bible - then you are dabbling in and opening yourself up to the demonic.

For there is one God and one mediator between God and mankind, the man Christ Jesus, who gave Himself as a ransom for all people. (1 Timothy 2:5)

Even if you don't believe in, know about or follow the beliefs behind a New Age practice, the fact that you submit yourself to a practitioner, even if sceptical, means that you are giving honour to and submitting yourself to the practitioner's beliefs and whatever is on their lives. Furthermore, even if one modality offered by a therapist seems harmless to you, in the New Age, virtually no practitioner operates in one mode of healing exclusively. They blend and combine modalities hoping to utilize as much power as possible. So you may think that you're going along 'just for a massage', but without your consent or knowledge , if the masseur also offers New Age modalities, you are likely to have some sort of 'energy' channelled through you by their silent prayers to the 'Universe', 'spirit guides' or false gods, as well as any number of other suspect extras. Here are some examples of the range of techniques offered by just a few practitioners I've come across in New Age magazines while writing this section:

- Energy kinesiology, acupressure, pre-dynastic Egyptian energy work, Egyptian healing rods, magnified healing, pyradym, healing codes
- Certified Reiki Master, Hypnotherapist, Spiritual Medium, Author of "Butterfly Within" and Teacher of Meditation and Spiritual Development Classes
- Doctor of Energetic Healing, Cellular Release, Meditative Coaching, Reflexology, Reiki Master, Thought Field Therapy, Core Transformation, Pranic Healing, Sharmanic Abilities
- Neuro-linguistic Programming, Body Talk Practitioner, Healing Angels Technique, Massage, Healing Touch, Reflexology
- Registered Nurse, Quantum Touch, Certified Theta Healer, Ordained Priestess
- Reiki Master, Iyengar/Tantra yoga instructor, Swedish / Shiatsu / Reflexology / Trager / Thai Yoga / NCR massage therapist, and is trained/certified in a variety of other healing modalities: Eastern Philosophy and Meditation, Shamanic Journeying, Soul Retrieval and Medicine Wheel work, Plant Spirit Medicine, Tensegrity, Remote Viewing, Belief Defusion (Shondra Johnston's work), Body M.A.T.H. (David Malin's Multidimension-

al Approaches to Healing) Landmark Education (EST), Family Constellations, Aka Dua, Reconnective Healing, Quantum Touch, Animal Communication, Gemstone Therapy, Aromatherapy, Flower Essence Therapy, Paganism, Herbalism, various detoxification protocols, and more.

My search for healing begins

The first modality I tried is called The Reconnection. The name for this modality was coined by American chiropractor, Eric Pearlman, who learned the method from a gypsy on the beach who convinced him to pay $333 to trace ancient grid lines over his body. The promises in the advertisement for The Reconnection seemed too good to be true, but I believed I needed the impossible to become real in order to be healed, so I chose to be open to something my logical mind was shaking its head at. The A3 ad I saw for The Reconnection promised that DNA could be repaired and limbs regrown, and there were stories of people healed of all sorts of problems, so it was hard to resist consideration. I ordered Pearlman's book *The Reconnection: Heal Others, Heal Yourself* and waded through the explanations about physics, universal energy and how Pearlman discovered he could bring supernatural healing to people. The Reconnection website sums up the belief behind the modality:

Originally the meridian lines (sometimes called acupuncture lines) on our bodies were connected to the grid lines that encircle the planet and cross at acknowledged power places such as Machu Picchu and Sedona. These grid lines were de-

signed to continue out and connect us to a vastly larger grid, tying us into the entire universe.

Each of our bodies contains our own set of energetic lines and points and, although only remnants of what they once were, these lines and points continue to serve as our interface with the universe. This interface is a channel that facilitates our communication of energy, light and information between large and small, macrocosm and microcosm, the universe and humankind. At one point in time, we became disconnected from these lines and lost the fullness of our inherent connection to the universe, distancing us from our previously rapid and expansive rate of evolution. The Reconnection brings in "new" axiatonal lines that reconnect us on a more powerful and evolved level than ever before. These lines are part of a timeless network of intelligence, a parallel-dimensional system that draws the basic energy for the renewal functions of the human body.[1]

Of all of the modalities I was considering, The Reconnection seemed to promise the fastest results. According to this modality, I just needed the earth's old grid lines traced over me so I would be realigned with God/the universe, and I would instantly be healed and restored to the way I had been, or maybe even better than before. These claims are far-fetched to a sane, questioning mind, I know - but seemed worth trying to a desperate, open mind bamboozled by pseudoscience and spiritualism.

I made an appointment to have a half hour healing session with a lady in Melbourne who is a full time practitioner. For half an hour, I lay on my back on a massage table and the lady, speaking in a whisper, told me about her experiences with angels as she walked around me, waving her hands a few inches above my body, occasionally saying things like, 'Tell me about your knee, there's something interesting happening around your knee.' (I had no problems with my knees!) I paid the lady $180 and she told me that to see a big change, I really needed to experience 'The Reconnection' – a full hour session where the ancient grid lines are drawn over the body. Although discouraged by the lack of difference, I decided to give this a try.

For the full 'Reconnection', I decided to try another practitioner, this time a man, who I decided to try simply because he was an English man and I like the English accent. This man only practised on weekends, having a regular job during the week. Again, as I lay on my back on a massage table, this man simply walked around me for an hour, tracing invisible lines a foot above my body. While lying there, feeling no sensation or difference whatsoever, I realised that this was a con and I actually felt worse than before because I knew I had to hand the man $333 for an hour long charade.

Disappointed, but undeterred, I continued my search. The second modality I tried was Quantum Touch. This modality was founded by Richard Gordon, a promoter of Life Force Science, who wrote the book *Quantum Touch: The Power to Heal*, which I ordered and read. Again, this is a New Age modality that aims to align itself with science, God and the energy of the universe. It is also nicknamed 'turbo charged Reiki'. Reiki is another very similar form of New Age energy healing. The Quantum Touch website describes the modality as:

...a powerful, yet easy to learn, method of natural healing (or energy healing). Everyone has the innate ability to help ourselves and others. The Quantum-Touch techniques teach us how to focus and amplify life-force energy (or Chi, Bioenergy, Prana) by combining various breathing and energy awareness exercises. QT energy healers learn to amplify and direct the

life-force energy, facilitating the body's own healing process. Our love has more impact than we can imagine; the possibilities are truly extraordinary.

Life-force energy is an effective tool for healing because of the principles of resonance and entrainment. In physics, entrainment theory is the process where two vibrating objects, vibrating at different speeds, start to vibrate at the same speed when energy is transferred between the two objects. Entrainment shows up in chemistry, neurology, biology, medicine, and more. For example, crickets will chirp in unison and fireflies will flash at the same time.

Using the Quantum-Touch techniques, we can create a high frequency of life-force energy. If we place this field of high energy around an area of pain, stress, inflammation, or disease, the body can entrain to the higher frequency, thus amplifying the body's ability to heal itself. [2]

The Quantum Touch advertisements made less extravagant promises than The Reconnection, and emphasised that it was a 'natural' technique to facilitate healing that is intrinsic to the body. It is also a modality that is promoted as something you can perform on yourself, so I decided to try it, thinking that it could save me some money. I attended a weekend workshop in Melbourne and took a friend along who suffered various aches and pains. What the practitioners do is quite simple: place hands on the area that needs healing, inhaling and exhaling deeply, breathing in the 'energy of the universe' through the length of your whole body, to raise your resonance, to apparently positively affect the resonance of the sick cells or organs to help them heal.

Apart from experiencing hyperventilation and dizziness from the deep, fast breathing, I achieved no lasting change or healing for any of my mental, emotional or physical problems.

My friend also received no lasting change, even though she felt the tension in her neck ease for a few hours. This lack of lasting results is a common characteristic of New Age healing. At best, if seeking healing through the New Age, you are likely to experience nothing or a placebo effect. If some type of healing were to be experienced, then it's important to be aware that the devil is a mimic and the Bible says he 'masquerades as an angel of light.' (2 Corinthians 11:14) Many illnesses and pains are caused by demons of sickness, and the devil can counterfeit healing by simply silencing or removing a spirit of pain for a time, to create the impression of healing. The pain or problem usually returns within a few hours, often worse, or later manifests as a different pain or illness elsewhere in the body. And so the person's search for healing continues and they remain in bondage to the modality they attribute their initial healing to and need to continually make appointments and pay in the desperate hope of achieving the same relief the following week.

It's worth pausing to point out that within Christian healing, healings can be lost, but the reasons why are different to the reasons why counterfeit New Age healing is often temporary. The following passage from the Bible explains why it is that some Christian healing might be lost:

But if I drive out demons by the finger of God, then the kingdom of God has come upon you. When a strong man, fully armed, guards his own house, his possessions are safe. But when someone stronger attacks and overpowers him, he takes away the armor in which the man trusted and divides up his plunder. Whoever is not with me is against me, and whoever does not gather with me scatters. When an impure spirit comes out of a person, it goes through arid places seeking rest and does not find

it. Then it says, 'I will return to the house I left.' When it arrives, it finds the house swept clean and put in order. Then it goes and takes seven other spirits more wicked than itself, and they go in and live there. And the final condition of that person is worse than the first.
(Luke 11: 20-26)

A person needs to be submitted to God to be sure of retaining their healing and not end up in a worse state, and they also need to understand their authority as a Christian to rebuff Satan's counter attacks.

The couple in Melbourne who led the QT workshop were lovely people, as are most people in the New Age. They were seeking healing and truth for themselves and also wanted to help others. They both had regular jobs during the week and offered QT healing sessions on weekends and they regularly attended seminars to learn other healing modalities. They also offered other New Age and occult practices such as crystal healing, meditation and Kabbalah. I tried a few sessions of healing with them, and I found comfort in telling them about some of what had happened to me, which I hadn't been able to confide in anyone else, but there really was no lasting difference to my level of inner torment.

Around the time of my healing journey, the book and movie *The Secret* came out. The author of *The Secret*, Rhonda Byrne, claims to have discovered the secret laws and principles of the universe, namely the 'Law of Attraction'. Byrne teaches that we need to simply ask and believe and we will receive all we desire from 'the Universe' – one of many interchangeable New Age names for their impersonal concept of God. *The Secret* teaches that the universe will answer and that what we focus on will grow. This is how the website for *The Secret* sums up its beliefs:

Money is magnetic energy. You are a magnet attracting to you all things, via the signal you are emitting through your thoughts and feelings. Discover how to become a powerful magnet for the creation of personal wealth.

Relationships can be completely transformed, no matter what it's like right now. Learn how to transform every single relationship you have in your life.

Concerned about your health? Explore ways to open yourself up and become a powerful magnet to wellness and health starting from wherever you are now.[3]

In the film of *The Secret*, which is based on the original book, we watch people who are examples of the law of attraction working to bring about all of their dreams. There are many tools taught by Byrne to help achieve whatever goals you have in life. These tools are common ones most people will be familiar with through popular self-help psychology. *The Secret* encourages people to create a visualisation board - a collage of images to help them focus on what they want in life. Positive thinking and positive affirmations are also key tools. Any techniques that can be used to help people fully imagine themselves and their ideal lives, while blocking out negatives, are utilised with *The Secret*.

Since becoming a Christian, I am constantly coming across new Christian principles and techniques for healing and counselling that have very close parallels in the New Age. It is clear that many people within the New Age borrow from Christianity, and this creates confusion amongst Christians who do not have a strong foundation in the Bible and are drawn into trying New Age practices thinking that there's no harm in them. There is also a danger that Christianity could unwittingly adopt New Age practices and bring them into church.

The Secret is a good example of a number of subtly deceptive practices and mindsets in the New Age. The book and film received broad publicity in the secular press around the world. *The Secret* is an example of a New Age philosophy of which people might ask, where is the harm in it? It's just positive thinking, isn't it? This is an example of the aspect of truth I mentioned earlier that you will often find in many New Age practices. On the surface level, *The Secret* seems to be about focusing on dreams for the future and positives. There is common sense truth in the fact that positive thinking and positive words do make a difference to a person's life. Very recently, scientists have been able to map what goes on in the brain when a person speaks or thinks positively or negatively. Research can now follow how words and thoughts trigger receptors and chemical reactions in the body which then measurably affect a person's health. Science has found it to be true that positive thinking and words can make a difference to a person's well being physically, emotionally and mentally. A book I recommend called *Who Switched off My Brain?: How to Control Toxic Thoughts and Emotions* by Dr Caroline Leaf, a Communication Pathologist who specialises in the field of cognitive neuroscience, is one of a number of recently published books which very simply explains the science behind positive thinking.[4]

However, what underpins *The Secret's* philosophy, and crosses the line from common sense to the spiritual, is a belief that the 'Universe' can be controlled by the sheer force of our will to carry out our desires. This concept of God does not accord with what the Bible teaches, so it is therefore a belief in a false god and a philosophy and practice that can expose us to demonic influence in our lives. The Bible does teach that we can pray to God and believe for anything that might constitute abundant life, but also that the answer to our prayers only comes through belief in the true God of the Bible, accessed through Jesus and His sacrifice on the cross, not through our own will. You might 'attract' all of your desires by believing that the universe will supply when you call on it to do so, but you are very likely to open a door to the devil - who will happily allow you a run of material success to secure your belief in a false god. All of the wealth in this world is not worth an eternity spent suffering in hell.

Esther and Jerry Hicks

While Rhonda Byrne claims to have discovered the secret of the universe, Esther and Jerry Hicks also claim to be the originators of the Law of Attraction. Esther Hicks channels the teachings of Abraham, the name given to the non-physical entities that speak through her. One of their best selling books is called *Ask and It Is Given*, a close paraphrasing of Biblical scripture from Matthew 7:7, *'Ask, seek and knock.'* In describing who or what Abraham-Hicks is, the word 'God' is never used, but every other characteristic normally attributed to God is made - plus the name Abraham has obvious biblical connotations. Here's an excerpt from their website:

Abraham has described themselves as "a group consciousness from the non-physical dimension." They have also said, "We are that which you are. You are the leading edge of that which we are. We are that which is at the heart of all religions."

Esther herself calls Abraham "infinite intelligence," and to Jerry they are "the purest form of love I've ever experienced."[5]

Some of the Abraham-Hicks teachings are summarised below and teach that we are divine in nature, which is why we can have whatever we ask for:

- *You Are a Physical Extension of That Which is Non-physical.*

29

- *You Are Here in This Body Because You Chose to Be Here.*
- *The Basis of Your Life is Freedom; the Purpose of Your Life is Joy.*
- *You Are a Creator; You Create With Your Every Thought.*
- *Anything That You Can Imagine is Yours to Be or Do or Have.*
- *You May Appropriately Depart Your Body Without Illness or Pain.*
- *You Can Not Die; You Are Everlasting Life.*[6]

It is important to be aware of popular New Age teachers, as their books and CDs have infiltrated the shelves of every New Age/self-help section in secular bookshops around the world. When we Christians meet someone who subscribes to the New Age, it is important to have some understanding of what these people believe, and the spiritual problems with their beliefs, so that we are not drawn into those beliefs; but also, so we are prepared to share Jesus. I don't recommend openly challenging people in the New Age or condemning or dismissing their beliefs, unless they openly challenge your beliefs as a Christian. But I do advocate an attitude of patience, understanding and love, while looking for an opportunity to share Jesus, planting a seed, and trusting the Holy Spirit to bring revelation and draw the person to want to know more.

As with *The Secret*, I purchased Hicks' books and attempted to 'attract' my health back. I even created a visualisation board. There are many clips on YouTube of Esther Hicks closing her eyes, nodding her head, breathing deeply and turning herself over to Abraham to speak through her. Audience members are told that they too can raise their vibrational frequency to match the frequency of their guide and connection to 'Source' so that they can reclaim their 'place as extension of Source energy. We want you to remember that you are eternally source energy, that you are mostly vibration.'[7]

The Abraham-Hicks teachings are classic New Age: there are no taboos, the purpose of life is pleasure and fun, and we are all one with 'Source' or 'God'. Although there is no apparent connection to Eastern religion in these teachings, they obviously parallel the Eastern philosophy; they teach that we are all gods and our journey and purpose in life is about coming to a realisation of this. What Esther Hicks does when she speaks as Abraham is become a medium for the demonic. A spirit of divination would be taking her over, and what is said is designed to lure and confuse people away from the truth.

If Satan presents us with so many spiritual options, it becomes very difficult to discern the truth, especially when we are tempted as Adam and Eve were to 'go beyond what God has appointed, and you shall become like God.' (Genesis 3:5) All forms of the occult present us with a similar temptation: will we act like humble children of the Heavenly Father and submit to God's wisdom in limiting our knowledge and power, or will we, like Adam and Eve, desire and chase after the false promise of knowledge that can make us wise and powerful like God?

Theta Healing

Theta Healing is another New Age modality that I tried. It makes big claims about what can be achieved with the therapy - including being able to reprogram your DNA, reverse ageing and heal any condition, as well as restoring or attracting perfect relationships and finances. As with many of the other modalities I tried, I ordered a book about Theta Healing first.

Theta Healing originated in America with a woman called Vianna Stibal. Stibal's website sums up the experience which led her to create Theta Healing:

In 1995 Vianna Stibal a Naturopath, Massage Therapist, and Intuitive Reader at the time, discovered that the way she did Readings could do an instant healing. Vianna, a mother of three young children was diagnosed with cancer that was quickly destroying her right femur. Everything she had tried using conventional and alternative medicine had failed. Then she discovered that the simple technique she used in Readings could heal. Her leg was instantaneously healed. She added this knowledge of ThetaHealing® to her sessions with clients and in the classes she was teaching. Curious to understand why the technique was working, Vianna solicited the help of a physicist and with an electrocephalograph discovered that the simple technique tapped Theta waves. Over many years of practicing the technique, Vianna believes the technique utilizes a Theta wave to achieve an instant healing. Through thousands of clients she discovered not only an amazing way to connect with the creative energy that moves in all things, but that this energy could change instantly Beliefs and Feelings that are linked to sickness.[8]

The therapy claims to be able to reprogram the unconscious mind by identifying and unblocking beliefs that are hindering healing. Stibal's name for her god is 'Creator Of All That Is.' I found an ad for Theta Healing in a free Melbourne health magazine and made an appointment to see a practitioner, Simon.

Simon presented as a charismatic, confident and articulate young man. Part of what drew me to try Simon as a practitioner above many others I could have chosen from in Melbourne was that his marketing was slick, with large, colourful advertisements in the free magazines, as well as an attractive and detailed website. More than this, Simon had been a corporate lawyer and it fascinated me that he had given that up to practise Theta Healing. Simon had discovered Theta Healing after becoming ill with a brain tumour and starting on his own search for healing. He was not healed through Theta Healing, but had the tumour removed in an operation. However, in his search through alternative therapies, he obviously found something he wanted to pursue as a career alternative to being a lawyer. Meeting Simon made me stop and think. Although I had been open to trying a number of New Age healing modalities, all of which make reference to a general, impersonal 'god', I was still struggling to believe there was a God - I saw no evidence of one, though I was open to being convinced otherwise. My attitude was: if I see evidence of God being real, then I will believe.

However, meeting Simon, a clever young man who believed in a god, challenged my concepts of people who believed in God. Up until that time, I had lumped all people who believed in God into one basket - Christians, New Agers, Hindus and Muslims were all equally batty, deluded and simple-minded to me.

I remember asking Simon, 'Do I need to believe in God to receive healing this way?'

He replied, 'Julie, when I had a brain tumour and attended a seminar on healing, I just decided "This weekend, I'm going to believe in God" and all I can say is that he is real.'

This was a turning point for me. I thought, 'Hmmm, give God a trial period. I can do that.' So I decided to believe in God wholeheartedly for one month, believing in Him and praying to Him as if He were real. I gave Him one month to demonstrate to me beyond a doubt that He was real.

I attended a few sessions of Theta Healing with Simon. I'll give you some idea of how a session ran. In one session, I was speaking to Simon about some of the symptoms of my extreme anxiety, particularly the burning, tight constricting feeling in my throat that ran down my oesophagus to my stomach. Simon said, 'It sounds like you might have been strangled to death in a former life. Let's ask the Universe.'

Simon directed me to stand facing north. He asked, 'Universe, was Julie strangled to death in a former life?' My body tipped forward to the north. This apparently indicated yes. This method is part of a range of techniques called muscle testing or applied body kinesiology, and is an example of a New Age diagnostic tool which is presented as a scientifically-verified physical assessment, many chiropractors use it, but in fact it has not stood up to scientific scrutiny. The exact mechanism of how it works is yet to be explained, as is the case with most forms of alternative and New Age therapy. The beliefs behind muscle testing or applied body kinesiology are the same as for Chinese practices such as acupuncture, which are deeply rooted in Eastern philosophy and religion. I will be discussing the spiritual danger of these practices later in the book.

The only explanation I can offer as to why I tipped forward is that a demonic force must have been working around me. I now know that when you call on an unseen power or energy, such as Simon's 'Creator', 'Universal Energy' or 'Source', you never know what spirit will answer, but it certainly will not be the Holy Spirit unless you are praying in Jesus' name and have committed your life to Him.

Once Simon established that I had been strangled to death in a former life, he set about trying to 'clear' my root fears associated with this apparent trauma, which would then heal my anxiety. A process of unravelling the past and searching for the root cause began. I was asked, 'What is the worst thing that could happen if you were strangled to death?' Whatever my answer, I would then be asked the same thing, 'What would be the worst thing that could happen to you then?' until we reached what Simon considered to be the rock bottom fear or belief. Once the root fear or belief that was blocking my healing was found, Simon 'tuned' into the theta level or 'seventh plane of existence' where 'Creator' was, to pray the fear or wrong belief away. To get to the theta level, Simon would sit still, close his eyes and flutter his eyelids at an unnaturally rapid rate. This process of questioning was repeated several times to deal with what he believed were a range of wrong beliefs I was holding on to that were supposedly hindering my healing.

Apart from being distracted for an hour during the session, I did not receive any lasting healing or change in my anxiety levels. The sessions were very expensive. My initial consultation was over $200 and every subsequent session was $150. I was so desperate to experience a change in my condition that I even tried Theta Healing sessions with several other practitioners in Australia - and even one in America, over the phone. If anything, my anxiety increased as I was going further into debt and becoming frustrated by the lack of results. Several of the practitioners said to me at the end of a session, 'There shouldn't be any reason for you to not be healed', which made me feel that there was something wrong with me, rather than the problem being with them and their bogus therapy. Each practitioner added their own personal touch and mix of other modalities to the therapy. One lady in Melbourne, who told me about having seen fairies in the forest, utilised her angel guides to help her 'read' my problem; but still, I found no relief.

Interestingly, and satisfyingly, in writing this section of my testimony, I researched Theta Healing and Simon on the internet, to see where things are at these days. I came across a number of websites by former Theta practitioners, including Simon's, which now disassociate themselves from Theta

Healing. Simon no longer practises Theta Healing, but has trademarked his own form of New Age healing which essentially looks just like Theta Healing, relabelled and repackaged.

When I first started writing my testimony at the end of 2010, Simon's website for his new therapy addressed his former work in Theta Healing and other forms of New Age therapy, stating that he and his wife:

> ...used to say there were already too many healing modalities. We spent more than 10 years searching for 'the answers'. We taught some techniques believing at first that they had the answers, and then realised they didn't. Our intuition told us that the highest path lay in combining the wisdom of many teachers and Masters...Because no existing healing or spiritual modality has all the answers, and because each of them limits its teachers.[9]

This paragraph no longer exists on his website, nor does any reference to Theta Healing. But in this paragraph, Simon summed up the ineffectiveness of all of the forms of healing he had previously tried, thereby exposing the fraudulence of New Age therapies and how so many 'new modalities' are created - by blending and varying what already exists and declaring that this new combination has the 'real' power. These are classic marketing strategies and the New Age is skilled at utilising them. Each year, New Age practitioners announce new revelations, new courses and training, and new 'scientific testing' to promote their modality as relevant, cutting edge and ever developing.

Simon was an internationally known personality within the Theta Healing world for several years. There was a need for him to delicately address and excuse his involvement in Theta Healing on his website as he shifted over to his own brand of therapy. As Simon established himself in his 'new' modality, the explanation on his website about why he is no longer involved in Theta Healing became briefer every few months, and now there are no references to Theta Healing on his website. However, some of his private and more scathing thoughts about Theta Healing can still be found on other former Theta practitioners' websites. On the website www.fraudthetahealing.com, several emails from Simon are included. Here's an excerpt from an email referring to the strange death of one former Theta healer, Anita, who had an acrimonious split with Vianna Stibal:

I knew Anita very well (she was my teacher and healer), and I was also very close friends with Vianna and Terry O'Connell at the time of the Anita's split from Theta. I was in Idaho at or around that time in 2005. I therefore heard three sides to the story.... I understand why Anita was so deeply hurt after what she invested in Vianna and her work. In fact it's probably exactly how I feel today after spending 24/7 for 5 years promoting Theta and building Theta in this country, only to realise I was promoting a pack of lies...

Anita was talented and deserved to be able to share her many gifts with the world. <u>She should not have died.</u> That's really our point. She shouldn't have died of pneumonia, or suicide or anything else. If Trisha or I caused any hurt then I'm sorry. We were perhaps consumed by a bigger picture, which is sheer shock and horror at what's going on in Theta-land.[10]

Simon now charges $475 for a 2.5 hour consultation for his new therapy. On his website homepage, Simon writes that his self-created therapy 'combines the strengths of many different modalities into one super technique.'[11]

Theta Healing does seem to be slowly imploding. Stibal has become embroiled in multiple legal cases against former practitioners who have criticised Theta Healing. She has even sued her husband for involving them in a car accident causing 'severe and debilitating' injuries to her body and mind that would continue 'hereafter.' This is ironic coming from a woman whose whole healing practice is based on her claim that she figured out how to heal herself from cancer instantly.[12]

Furthermore, contradictions and questions started to be raised about the truth of Vianna's personal testimony of healing from cancer, for which no convincing evidence has ever been presented. The validity of Stibal's qualifications and claims to be a naturopathic doctor are also a concern as there is no register of her studying for such a degree. Regular errors in her understanding of even basic diseases add weight to the suspicion that many of her claims are fraudulent. Plagiarism from medical texts has been found in her books.[13]

Most scathing of all the former practitioners openly damning Theta Healing is Tricia Howell. She turned her original website, once used to promote her practice as a Theta healer, over to exposing Theta Healing as an 'insidious cult'. Eventually, after a lengthy legal battle, the web address was awarded to Vianna Stibal and again promotes Theta Healing. But Howell has started another website, www.fraudthetahealing. com, to continue exposing what she sees as disturbing spiritual problems with Theta Healing. Here are some excerpts from what Tricia Howell has to say about the dangers of Theta Healing:

Theta Healing is a subtle cult founded in the late 1990's in Idaho Falls, Idaho by a charismatic guru-like woman, Vianna Stibal. Vianna—with the help of her husband Guy Stibal, a dark shaman—befriended an entity called Creator. Vianna has a special relationship with Creator, a being she claims is God but which has been experienced by hundreds of former Theta Healers as a dark entity that subtly takes some of practition-

ers' energy in exchange for "healings." Theta Healing is both dangerous to practitioners and largely ineffective for recipients (though it can accomplish some with the placebo effect).

Howell makes frightening claims about what has happened to many former Theta Healers who have criticised Stibal:

In fact, several Theta Healers close to Vianna have ended up unexpectedly dead within a short time after have a falling out with her. I myself came down with severe metastatic breast cancer overnight after speaking the truth about the dark side of Theta Healing. I am the only one I know of who is still alive after Guy Stibal performed daily nearly a year of dark rituals against me. My illness—which all my doctors say is the most aggressive breast cancer they've ever seen—is getting better after we finally changed my "spiritual address" so that Guy could no longer blow black smoke into my chest. This was after months in which Vianna and Guy kept re-hooking me to Creator so as to harm me. I was susceptible to this because I had completely opened myself to Creator as result as my Theta Healing training.

During the two years I was practicing Theta Healing nearly full-time, the following occurred:

- *My hair went from no gray to about half gray.*
- *I gained 25 pounds while actually eating less and exercising more than before.*
- *I experienced rapid disc degeneration in my lower back, making it hard sometimes to even lift my leg enough to put on my pants and socks.*
- *I felt progressively more fatigued and could not work at the pace I used to (though I still worked at a much faster pace than most people).*
- *My fibroid tumors ballooned out extraordinarily rapidly—from being barely detectable on an ultrasound to*

being together the size of a small baby when they were removed August 2008.

- *My psoriasis failed to improve and in some ways got worse, despite extensive Theta Healing on it.*
- *I had increasing constipation.*
- *I experienced more sickness than I ever had in my life previously. (I had never been before a person to get colds, flus, upset stomach, etc.)*
- *I developed full-blown breast cancer the size of a cantaloupe in my left breast and lymph nodes literally over night. All doctors I consulted with said this is medically impossible. It should have taken 5-10 years to grow to that size. (A thorough gynecological exam just a few months before found my breasts to be totally normal.) I consulted with 4 psychics without telling them anything about me. They all said it was manifested in me by a healer couple in Idaho who wanted me dead. By the way, the left breast is the one where my husband Dean and numerous others saw the Creator attachment coming into me.*[14]

I have given time to revealing some of the storm surrounding Theta Healing because there is a lot to learn about the dangers of New Age healing here. New Age practitioners themselves denounce the modality as fraudulent and demonic. Tricia Howell reveals the dark side and frightening consequences of being involved with the practice and of having willingly opened herself to a destructive spiritual entity, which at first appeared to be good. However, both Simon and Tricia Howell continue to practise other forms of New Age healing, even though both try hard to validate what they are now involved with as being scientifically verified. All forms of New Age healing deal with darkness, but most people in the New Age are deluded in believing that they are operating with the same source of light and power that we Christians are with Jesus; they are blind to seeing that they are part of the occult. However, their ignorance doesn't mitigate the dangers associated with deceptively milder modes of New Age healing compared to explicit occult practices. Whenever you submit yourself to a treatment with someone who practices New Age healing, you risk exposing yourself to the demonic.

Many other New Age practices I tried will be discussed later in the book.

MY SALVATION

Becoming frustrated with the lack of results and the thousands of dollars it was costing me in my fruitless search for healing through Theta Healing, I started wondering why it was, that if there were a God and He created everything and knew everything, that I had to pay money for someone to pray to Him for me. The vague notions about God I was continually confronted with in the New Age were also a frustration because I felt the need for rules and definite information about God that I could live by that might help me in my healing. I decided that if I was going to believe in God for a month, I'd find out what the Bible had to say about Him. I had tried to read the Bible several times before as an intellectual exercise. I had set out to read it from cover to cover, as I would read other books, and found that I fell asleep only a few pages into Genesis. I don't recall anyone ever telling me to start reading the New Testament first or that the Bible didn't have to be read in the chronological order of its books. Thankfully, though, on this occasion when I was genuinely seeking to find out if God was real, I had a small red Gideons New Testament that I had souvenired six or seven years before when Gideons International came to the school where I was teaching to distribute them to students.

One afternoon, I took my dusty little Bible home from work. I opened to the index page, which in a Gideons Bible is titled 'Where to find help, when…' I scanned down the list and just about everything on the list described my situation: Afraid, anxious, defeated, depressed, facing a crisis, needing peace, needing rules for living, and that was just the first page! I turned to the corresponding pages of scripture listed beside the issues and these are some of the first lines I read:

I sought the Lord, and He heard me, and delivered me from all my fears. (Psalm 34:4 Gideon)

Be anxious for nothing, but in everything by prayer and supplication, with thanksgiving, let your requests be made known to God. And the peace of God, which surpasses all understanding, will guard your hearts and minds through Christ Jesus. (Philippians 4: 6-7 Gideon)

The Lord shall preserve you from all evil; He shall preserve your soul. (Psalm 121:7 Gideon)

Something switched inside me and my heart thumped wildly and seemed to be somersaulting. The words spoke straight to me and my situation. They were the exact words I needed to hear and they comforted me deeply. I thought, 'Could this be real? Is God real?'

I started to read The Gospel of Matthew. Only a few chapters into the Gospel, I just simply, instantly understood that what I was reading was true, and I was a believer. My spiritual eyes were suddenly opened, just like in the song 'Amazing Grace' - 'I once was lost, but now am found; was blind, but now I see.'

After many months of trauma and torment, I had found peace.

I felt overwhelmed by a strange sensation of calm, comfort and serenity and later realised that the Holy Spirit, the presence of God, had come over me.

As I read through the Gospel of Matthew, God's promises for healing, abundant life on earth and eternal life through belief in Jesus leapt off the page at me and I cried tears of relief. I understood what the Bible being a 'Living Word' meant – it's supernatural and 'speaks' to you because it is God-breathed and Spirit-inspired. This is something you can't understand until you experience and you can't experience until you are open to God.

Spiritual revelation was a new and startling experience to me. I wish someone had tried to explain to me earlier that there was such an experience – a 'knowing' certainty you have upon realising the reality of Jesus. My instant conversion was outside logic. It is hard to imagine or comprehend an experience that is outside anything else you've experienced. For me, the realisations that Jesus is real, that heaven and hell are real places and that the Bible is truth, were instantly planted in me as unshakeable certainties. This realisation was certainly not the result of any brain-washing or wishful thinking. I hadn't wanted to believe in Jesus or the Bible. The only thing I can liken my spiritual revelation to is a computer download. One minute you don't believe in God and the next minute you not only believe, but understand new things which are outside experience or learnt knowledge.

*I received my message from no human source, and no one
taught me. Instead, I received it by direct revelation from
Jesus Christ.* (Galatians 1:12 NLT)

My understanding of the 'big picture' of life and where I
stood spiritually was clear to me: when I didn't know Jesus, I
was on my way to hell for eternity, but now that I had found
Jesus, I was destined for eternal life in heaven – a destiny
which God wants for every person and had always intended
from the start of creation before Adam and Eve disobeyed God
and brought sin into the world. This understanding was beyond the knowledge I could gain in reading half a Gospel. I
just 'knew' and all of my past doubts and questions dissolved.

This was my experience of being 'born again.' This phrase
'born again' is another Christian phrase I'd heard before, but
didn't understand. Being 'born again' is something that hap-
pens when a person surrenders their life to Jesus and confesses
Him as their Lord. The Holy Spirit of God comes and lives in
the believer's heart. The presence of the Holy Spirit in your
life brings guidance and prompting, which gently transforms
you to live and behave in a more Godly way. The measure
and speed at which this transformation takes place often cor-
relates with how closely we listen to and embrace the leading
of the Holy Spirit, but God is sovereign and many people are
transformed and set free instantly from issues they've struggled with all their lives.

*Therefore, if anyone is in Christ, he is a new creation;
the old has gone, the new has come!* (2 Corinthians 5:17)

For some time after my salvation, I was in a state of shock.
I realised how close I had come to spending eternity tormented
in hell. How could I not have known about this before? Why

hadn't anyone tried harder to tell me about Jesus? Why weren't more Christians fulfilling Jesus' commission to go out into the world and preach the Gospel? Why weren't Christians living in greater victory? I panicked about all my unsaved family and friends and all of the good people in the world who would go to hell because they have never stood still long enough to hear about what the Bible says about heaven and hell.

I thought about my friends who were Christians and sadly reflected that they had never braved my cynicism to try to share that Jesus is real. I would almost certainly have scoffed and dismissed what they had to say in a proud display of un-belief, but it still would have been a seed planted in me that the Holy Spirit could have drawn on later, when my guard was down and I was openly searching. If someone had offered to pray for me or if I'd been told that Jesus heals and the church prays for people, it would have been filed away in my mind and possibly something I could have turned to earlier when my world fell apart.

I thought of my former boyfriend, Stephen. We went out together for seven years. His parents were pastors, yet they never once witnessed to me about Jesus or told me about heav-en and hell and how to make sure I was going to heaven, which is succinctly summed up in Romans 10:9:

If you declare with your mouth, 'Jesus is Lord,' and be-lieve in your heart that God raised Him from the dead, you will be saved.

So now, whenever I share my testimony, I encourage Chris-tians that they must tell people about Jesus and how to be sure to get to heaven. At the very least, every Christian has a re-sponsibility to witness to their friends and family who don't know Jesus. Strangers from the Christian Union who tried to approach me at university didn't stand much chance in witnessing to me, but friends and family who had access to my ear could have braved my scorn to plant a seed of truth about Jesus.

Before I was saved, any time I blasphemed against God, a little voice in my head always said, 'But what if? What if?' There's a God-sized hole in our hearts that only the Holy Spirit can fill when we receive Jesus. Every time we share what Jesus has done for us, or offer to pray for someone, or try to tell someone about heaven, we give an opportunity for the Holy Spirit to tug on and open a person's heart. Plus you give them knowledge of where they can turn when things spiral out of control in their lives and seem beyond hope or human mending.

Another initial reaction I had to my conversion was, 'Oh no! Now I'm a daggy Christian!' But I didn't really care. I thought it would serve me right if I were mocked or shunned for becoming a Christian. If living with the label of being a 'Christian' and having to put up with smirks and jibes from others who hadn't yet had a revelation about Jesus was the price to pay to have found peace like I'd never known before, then that was a very small cost compared to the rewards. I am saved and my eternal home in heaven is secure. Nothing, absolutely nothing, is worth more than that.

In finding this peace, my healing had begun.

Claiming God's promises for healing

God's promises for my life unfolded as I read the New Testament. I knew that I had found what I was looking for – healing, peace and restoration. Better than that, I had stumbled upon truth and the real God – Jesus - something I wasn't expecting or looking for. Jesus and the peace and eternal life only He can bring are what everyone is ultimately searching for, but many are too proud and logical to be open to, as I had been. For too long, I had rejected the idea of God, especially the Christian view, because of misconceptions I held that were based on ignorant impressions formed from a handful of random experiences and observations of Christians. When I was an atheist, I knew there were things Christians believed that meant you would have to change or give up a lot of things in life and I perceived this as a loss of liberty. However, after I was saved, I saw things from a completely new angle – God's perspective. For example, my negative attitude towards men and marriage changed. At the time when I became a Christian, I still thought that it would suit me better not to marry, but my mind was open to understanding the value of the commitment of marriage and the beauty of celibacy before marriage. Since then, I've found, many times, that healing can come through a change of perspective and looking at a situation from God's perspective.

I also discovered that you can be healed reading the Bible and claiming its promises and declaring them out loud. This is how I received most of my healing from panic attacks, anxiety, fears and the effects these conditions had on my immune system, sleep and health in general. Some of my favourite scriptures are:

If you believe, you will receive whatever you ask for in prayer. (Matthew 21:22)

Jesus looked at them and said, 'With man this is impossible, but with God all things are possible.'
(Matthew 19:26)

Ask, and it will be given to you; seek, and you will find; knock, and it will be opened to you. For everyone who asks receives; he who seeks finds; and to him who knocks, the door will be opened. (Matthew 7:7-8)

Come to me, all you who are weary and burdened, and I will give you rest. (Matthew 11:28)

For God has not given us a spirit of fear and timidity, but of power, love, and self-discipline. (2 Timothy 1:7 NLT)

I highlighted these verses and many others in my little red Gideons New Testament. I repeatedly read and spoke them aloud, claiming them for myself. Being a list maker, I drew up a long list of all of the things I wanted healed mentally, emotionally and physically. Every morning and night, I held up my list to heaven and prayed, declaring that I refused to accept these things in my life and that by Jesus' stripes I was healed. I also drew up a list of all of the things I did want in my life, and thanked Jesus that He came to bring me 'life more abundantly' and that I would receive whatever I asked for in prayer because I believed in Him. Each time I prayed or read the Bible, I felt the presence of God come and surround me like a cocoon of peace and calm. I had an image in my mind of being cradled in God's arms. I felt better and freer each day. Every two weeks or so, I would reassess my lists and realised that several things were no longer issues for me, so I struck them off. The Holy Spirit would then show me other things to add to my lists and the process continued and still does today, though my list is short and the issues relatively minor. Thank you, Jesus!

> *I led them with cords of human kindness, with ties of love.*
> *To them I was like one who lifts a little child to the cheek,*
> *and I bent down to feed them.* (Hosea 11:4)

STRANGE SPIRITUAL ENCOUNTERS

Early in my salvation, strange things started happening around me, especially at night, that made me aware of how real the spirit world is. I remember closing my eyes one evening as I was reading the Bible and reflecting on what I had just read when an audible voice said, 'You need to clear your fourth chakra.' Simultaneously, I also saw a vision of a green light, like the pilot light in an oven. Spooked, I sat bolt upright and looked around. 'Chakras? Chakras?' I thought, 'God doesn't talk about chakras!' I understood that some demonic spirit was trying to lure me back into the New Age. A spiritual tug of war seemed to begin in my life, but Jesus had already won.

For a season, I had a series of strange dreams and visions wake me at night, and I couldn't figure out what they meant or if they were from God or Satan. I remember the first vision very clearly. In the middle of the night, I was shaken awake and watched, like a movie in my mind, a night sky with clouds passing over a full moon. Something was approaching from the distance and I eventually saw that it was a white horse, not a unicorn. These visions left me baffled and disturbed my sleep.

The most unpleasant experience that started at this time was a dark figure that came and overshadowed me as I slept, waking me. I was paralysed with fear and could not move my limbs or speak. All I could do was scream out to Jesus in my mind and struggle to regain movement. Each experience would last about two minutes, and this happened almost every second night. Even though I prayed, bound and rebuked every evil spirit I could think of before I went to bed, still it came. I think it was a spirit of fear. Soon, I stopped being afraid of the presence: it wasn't hurting me or touching me. Instead, I became annoyed and angry and searched the scriptures for advice on how to deal with demons and fear.

During this time, I learned how real the spirit world is and became aware of how I had exposed myself to demonic forces by dabbling in the New Age. Looking back, I now see that this period of spiritual battle was preparing me for the ministry I now share with my husband, John, in praying for healing and deliverance. My spiritual authority increased over this time and my fear of demonic powers disappeared, replaced by righteous anger. Each month, the night visits and paralysis became shorter and less frequent, and I gained more control over my body and voice, but it took two years for the night visits to end completely. There were times when I wondered if I were losing my mind and I told no one about the experiences because I was sure they would have thought I was going crazy.

GOING TO CHURCH

After a month or two of reading the New Testament at home, praying to Jesus for my healing and highlighting and claiming God's promises for healing, I was almost completely free of panic attacks and anxiety. I started to think about going to church. A scripture from Hebrews 10:25 was on my mind, 'Let us not give up meeting together, as some are in the habit of doing, but let us encourage one another—and all the more as you see the Day approaching.' I had a sense that God wanted me to go to church. I realised that I was spiritually limiting myself by trying to figure out God, the Bible and Christian life at home alone. However, as I had only ever stepped foot in traditional churches a few times for christenings, weddings, funerals, Christmas and Easter, I wasn't convinced that I would fit in or enjoy church, which to me seemed like near obsolete clubs for old ladies.

One day, on a whim, I typed into Google 'healing miracles.' The very first article that came up listed a string of miracles and named the Catholic Charismatic Renewal (CCR) as a source of these testimonies. There was also a mention of a Charismatic Community in London named the Cor et Lumen Christi Community and its leader, Damian Stayne, who went on mission trips to Africa and saw many miracles. I was amazed and excited by what I was reading.

I Googled 'Catholic Charismatic Renewal' to find out what it was about. The first website I came to was for a church in Melbourne which was a main centre for the CCR in Australia. I could see that the church held several healing services each week. Looking around the site, I saw many healing events listed. I knew from reading the New Testament and my own experience over the past months that Jesus still heals, but this was the first time I had come across information about other Christians, and the church, believing for healing and miracles today.

I clicked on the latest newsletters and read a report about a man from Geelong praying with his prayer group for a lady who was blinded in an eye by a garden stake, who doctors had said would never get her sight back. The prayer group prayed for her and she was totally healed, as was another lady in the group who had been diagnosed with a terminal illness. I also read in the newsletter that the main speaker for the National CCR Conference that year was Damian Stayne, so I looked him up on the internet. His community's website listed miracles the group saw on their mission trips to Africa – blind eyes opening, the lame walking and the dead being raised. I was a little stunned and overwhelmed by what I'd stumbled across.

The next morning, I wondered if I'd dreamt about these miracles, but I checked the internet again and saw that the websites were real and the news of the miracles was still there. I decided immediately that I would attend the National CCR Conference which was in Canberra around Easter, only a month away. I could not wait to witness miracles!

In the month before going to Canberra, I decided I wanted to see what went on at the Charismatic church in Melbourne, but I was a little nervous about going into unknown territory. I phoned the church to ask about the healing services and to see if I was welcome to attend. Mary, the receptionist, witnessed to me about her own healing from a bladder condition that several operations could not fix. A charismatic doctor and minister from Malta, Dr John Bonnici, prayed for her the year before and she was instantly healed.

I decided that I would drive past the church at the time a

service was about to start, just to check out where it was and see what type of people attended, but I was not intending to go in. As I drove slowly past St Augustine's Church on Bourke Street in Melbourne, a car pulled out right at the front of the church. I drove into the parking space. I sat in my car observing people arriving and I could hear music and singing inside. Curiosity got the better of me and I decided to stick my head in the door to see what the church was like inside.

As soon as I set foot in the church, the Holy Spirit overwhelmed me and it felt like I was walking through water, the atmosphere was so thick with God's presence. Tears started rolling down my face uncontrollably, so I found a place to sit at the side of the church towards the back. I remember the worship team was singing 'Come Holy Spirit Fall Afresh on Me.' At the end of each worship song, the musicians and many people in the church sang their own words which I couldn't understand, but which were soothing to hear. After a few songs, it dawned on me that they were 'singing in tongues,' something I only vaguely knew about from reading the New Testament. I also started to notice that anytime someone said or sang 'Holy Spirit', which they did about every minute, I had a fresh burst of tears. I was mortified when, in his welcome, the priest said, 'Turn to your neighbours and say hello.' My neighbours on the pew didn't know how to take me with tears streaming down my face as I tried to smile at them and offered my hand. To this day, I still have a conditioned dread of the 'greet your neighbour time' at the start of a service because for about the first two years of attending church, I had tears running down my face which I couldn't control and which had nothing to do with my emotions: I was happy and peaceful, crying but not sobbing. Someone later told me I had the 'Gift of Tears.' I still struggle to hold back tears when anyone speaks of the Holy Spirit, when worship is particularly anointed, when I share what Jesus has done for me and also when I pray for people, especially for healing of emotions. I'd love to swap this 'gift' for another one, but I think it's there to keep me humble.

Looking around the church, I could see that the congregation was a mixed group of people from all nationalities. There were many elderly and Asian people, and also a fair number of people who looked like they were living roughly, on drugs and mentally ill. St Augustine's has a street ministry to the homeless. Although I felt self-conscious and a bit uncomfortable at first to be in such unfamiliar surroundings, it seemed right and humbling for me to be standing amongst other broken people who were looking to God to restore them.

The priest leading the service that day, Father Andrew Heredia, was filling in for the usual priest, who was on holiday. Father Andrew is a retired Franciscan priest who has recently turned 90, but he was in his 80s when I first met him. Originally from the Czech Republic, his message that day was his testimony about how Jesus healed his blind eyes when he was a little boy. When he was seven, he and his friends tied bottles to a tree and smashed them with sticks. Shattered glass went into his eyes, scratching and blinding them. Doctors said that he would never see again because of the scarring, but the church prayed for him and his vision was perfectly restored. These early testimonies had a powerful effect on me, bringing me great encouragement and building my faith.

When it came time to be prayed for, I went to the front with everyone else and was anointed with oil on my palms and forehead. After the service, Father Andrew stood at the door to farewell everyone. For about ten minutes, no one left the church as they stayed to drink tea and enjoy fellowship. I was the first to leave, but I paused at the door to thank Father Andrew and let him know that his was the first church service

I had attended after finding Jesus. He was very moved by this and spent ten minutes encouraging me, praying for me and blessing me. Over the next year and a half, I attended many Charismatic seminars and meetings and Father Andrew always went out of his way to speak with me and pray for me.

As I left my first visit to church as a Christian, I felt a foot taller, as though a huge weight had been lifted from me, and I was full of peace and joy. While I had experienced a beautiful, comforting presence of the Holy Spirit come over me at home alone, the presence of God is definitely much stronger where people come together to worship and seek God.

I recall feeling quite dazed for some time after turning to Jesus and learning of miracles. First, I was in shock at the realisation that I had come close to going to hell and that no one close to me had ever taken the time to witness to me about Jesus and heaven and hell. It was as though I had stumbled upon a parallel universe where normal looking people that you pass on the street got up to strange things such as praying for miracles, that I had never been aware of before. I couldn't believe I had lived so long without knowing about Jesus and His power.

READING ABOUT HEALING AND DELIVERANCE

Desiring more information on Christian healing, I started to search for resources. Some of the earliest books and CDs I came across were the most influential and powerful. Derek Prince's teaching was amongst the first I came across, and I still think it's the most powerful, best written and most practical teaching on healing and deliverance available. I own just about all of Prince's books and CDs.

Each time a new book or CD arrived in the mail, I would stay up until the early hours of the morning finishing them in one sitting. I learnt a lot about the spirit world and spiritual authority through Prince's teachings and I immediately applied what I learnt and prayed for myself more confidently, binding and casting out any spirits I thought may have been hanging around. Up until then, I had been declaring Bible scriptures on healing aloud over my life and I was experiencing great healing, especially of my emotions. With Prince's teachings, I discovered that you can deliver yourself from demonic strongholds, and I had greater and faster breakthroughs in my healing by rebuking demonic forces than I did with just confessing scripture.[15] Confessing scripture aloud helped to renew my mind and attitudes to God's Word and truth and position me to receive my legal inheritance as a Christian. It was in binding demonic forces and releasing the healing anointing over my life, in Jesus' name, that I found faster progress.

I tell you the truth, whatever you forbid on earth will be forbidden in heaven, and whatever you permit on earth will be permitted in heaven. (Matthew 18:18 NLT)

Reading the New Testament had given me a spiritual revelation about Satan's plots and methods, and a righteous anger stirred in me to rebuke these things and free myself in Jesus' name from every effect and bit of damage the trap I had fallen into had brought.

Other books that were powerful tools in my early days were some guided prayer booklets by Catholic priest Father Robert de Grandis.[16] No one had taught me how to pray, so I just went with my instincts for about the first two months of my salvation. Reading through these prayer booklets by Father de Grandis confirmed that I was on the right track with my prayers, but they also showed me a huge range of other things I could pray for to help with the healing process, things such as generational curses, word curses, the healing of memories, healing of self-image, and so on. I prayed through many of these prayers, inserting my own circumstances, for about an hour every morning and an hour every evening. Within a month or so, the bulk of my emotional trauma was completely gone. Through this process, I learned the power of specific and persistent prayer.

I also learnt the power of worshipping and praising God to bring peace. Many people looking in on the church from the outside think that what we experience in church when we're worshipping God together is some sort of collective emotional high. Of course there is comfort and a sense of strength to be found in unity, but there's much more taking place during worship than that. I have met several people who have the spiritual gift of seeing in the spirit realm, for example, so they can see angels and demons. During worship, they see that demons flee outside the church door, because they cannot bear to hear God praised. If you've never tried pausing to praise God for 5-10 minutes when going through a tough time, then I encourage you to try it. At first it may feel and seem counter intuitive, especially when you're feeling low, tired or angry, but then many principles of God go against intuition because they oppose things of the flesh to break into the spiritual. Isaiah 61:3 prescribes that we put on the 'garment of praise instead of a spirit of despair.' That is, you can choose to praise God, even if you feel down, and the heaviness over you will lift. It works because Jesus is real, and biblical principles hold truth and supernatural power.

In using these tools of spiritual warfare, sooner or later, you will stop being oppressed and disturbed by demons that try to bring you down, because they must bow to the name of Jesus. Bombarding evil spirits with worship, and with forceful, authoritative prayer, will eventually drive them away from you for good.

FORGIVENESS AND HEALING

The importance and power of forgiveness also stood out very clearly in the Bible and in the books I was reading on healing as something that was essential to receiving answers to my prayers for healing, 'And when you stand praying, if you hold anything against anyone, forgive him, so that your Father in heaven may forgive you your sins.' (Mark 11:25)

There was someone that I held responsible for the trauma I had been through. The anguish that stirred in my mind and emotions every time I thought over the nightmarish sequence of events caused torment and physical sickness in my stomach and throat. At that point, I could not envisage the day when I would ever feel free from feelings of bitterness, vengeance, regret and blame for what this person had done. However, being determined to receive total healing through Jesus, as fast as possible, I forced myself to obey God and forgive this person.

I recall the first time I prayed a prayer to forgive this person - I was physically unable to open my mouth or get the words out - something was stopping me and constricting my throat. I felt that a demonic spirit must have been trying to prevent me from saying the prayer to forgive because the result of doing so would be powerful. This made me all the more determined to thwart the devil and forgive, so I kept persisting in repeating the prayer and forcing the words of forgiveness out, until my throat and mouth loosened and I could say the prayer freely.

After I had prayed to forgive, I found that my mind was bombarded more often than before with tormenting thoughts of what had happened to me. Every 15 minutes or so, bitter memories and feelings rose up. Not wanting to take the unforgiveness back, I arrested the thoughts and refused to let them cycle in my mind and I said out loud every time the thoughts tried to torment me, 'No, I have forgiven_____ and Jesus I release this person to you for blessing and healing and I ask you to forgive me, heal me and my memories and emotions, as fast as you can, thanks Lord.'

This regular bombardment of negative thoughts continued for about two weeks and I was exhausted by the constant effort to rebuff them. Thankfully, after two weeks, the regularity of the tormenting thoughts started to dissipate and within two months they stopped. It was then that I realised that the painful memories and emotions associated with what had happened to me were gone. It was an unexpected surprise and relief - the past traumatic events had become a neutral memory, as though they had happened to someone else. God had given me a new perspective on my situation: what I had considered the worst thing that had ever happened to me, now appeared as a blessing because it had brought me into relationship with Jesus and secured my eternal home in heaven with Him. It had taken something extreme to bring me to this revelation.

My whole process of forgiveness was not easy - it cost me great effort and self-control - but through it I have learned that God is faithful and that if we obey His principles, healing and freedom come, 'If you abide in me, and my words abide in you, ask whatever you wish, and it will be done for you.' (John 15:7 ESV)

In my ministry with John, I often counsel people who aren't getting a breakthrough in their healing in the prayer queue, to determine the reason for the hindrance. Holding unforgiveness is one of the most common blockages to receiving healing that we see in our ministry. Once I explain to people that forgiveness is a decision to obey God and release those who have hurt them to Him and let go of the past, I lead them through a prayer to forgive. Many times I have witnessed others have difficulty speaking the prayer out loud, just as I did. I have also seen people dramatically and instantly healed physically and emotionally as they say the prayer out loud. A copy of the prayer that I lead people through is at the back of the book.

In addition to receiving healing for my mind and emotions through declaring healing scripture, praying persistently, worshipping God and applying His principles for living, I have also been healed physically through the laying on of hands and being in the atmosphere of healing meetings. Some healings have been instant and others have been progressive as I continued to seek God and pursue ministries with an anointing for healing. I have also laid hands on myself and commanded healing may times with powerful effect.

Being baptised in the Holy Spirit

I didn't fully understand what I was getting myself into when I impulsively registered to attend the four day National CCR Conference in Canberra. Essentially, it's a time for several hundred leaders of the Charismatic Renewal around Australia to come together and sit under teaching on Gifts of the Spirit, to discuss what's been happening in their regions and plan for the future. So there I was, saved for only a few months, having attended a handful of church services, sitting amongst priests, nuns, lay ministers and prayer leaders.

The key speaker for the event was Damian Stayne, the man who saw miracles. He taught on the Gifts of Healing for a few days and shared many testimonies.

On one of the mornings, Damien said he was going to pray for Baptism of the Holy Spirit. I didn't fully understand what this meant, but from reading the Book of Acts in the Bible, I knew it meant receiving more from God, and I was determined to receive as much from God as possible. So, when Damien asked for anyone who would like to be baptised in the Holy Spirit to stand, up I stood. He then asked us to raise our hands to God. As I was new to all of these things, I didn't feel fully comfortable raising my hands high, so I stood with my arms upturned at waist height.

Damien started to pray and I closed my eyes.

Almost immediately, a ball of bright light came and hovered about a metre above me to the left. I could see the ball of light and its intense brightness even though I had my eyes closed. Heat and the presence of God radiated through me in waves and my head was filled with a voice repeating, 'I love you, I love you, I love you' continuously. Overwhelmed, I wept heavily. I could hear others in the room crying and falling down and some were being delivered. I wanted to reach up to touch the light and as I raised my hands higher, the light became even brighter, until my arms were fully raised, praising God. I stood like this for an hour, locked in a conversation with God, not wanting to be the one to break such a beautiful encounter. The Holy Spirit continued to saturate me and the voice continued to flood me with 'I love you' and I continued to cry. After an hour I still hadn't opened my eyes. I couldn't hear anyone else in the room and was sure that they'd all gone to lunch. I opened my eyes for a second and to my surprise, everyone was still in the room, silently sitting in the presence of the Lord. I closed my eyes again and the light, heat and 'I love you' were still there. Then I had a revelation: God's love and presence are always with me, so I sat down. I had received an understanding of one of the names given to Jesus in the Bible: Immanuel, meaning 'God with us.'

When I walked outside after this extraordinary experience, I realised that I couldn't feel my feet on the ground. It felt like I was floating and gliding. I had no sense of the weight of my body. It was a frosty day in Canberra, but the sun was out, and I marvelled at the beauty of the sky and trees, as though I were seeing them for the first time. I thought, 'Wow! Wow! Look how beautiful everything is!' I felt pure, overwhelming joy, love and appreciation for all things. My mind was crystal clear. This blissful state lasted for two days and I knew that this was a foretaste of how things will be in heaven.

After being baptised in the Holy Spirit, the conviction, guiding hand and voice of the Holy Spirit became much stronger and clearer in my life. There were a few areas of my life that needed to be straightened out and I felt a greater urgency to deal with them. Plans and changes for my future also formed as definite resolves in my mind.

OBEYING GOD AND DEALING WITH SIN

The Bible is quite clear about sin and how it separates us from God and can be an obstacle to the power of God touching us:

Or do you not know that the unrighteous will not inherit the kingdom of God? Do not be deceived: neither the sexually immoral, nor idolaters, nor adulterers, nor men who practice homosexuality, nor thieves, nor the greedy, nor drunkards, nor revilers, nor swindlers will inherit the kingdom of God. (1 Corinthians 6:9-10 ESV)

I wanted very much to put everything in my life right with God, be close to Him, cleanse myself from all sin, be able to receive a full measure of His blessing and healing power, and be sure of eternity in heaven with Jesus.

One particular area in my life that I knew needed to be addressed was my relationship with my boyfriend at the time. The relationship was going nowhere and I wanted it to end. However, I hesitated to end the relationship, even though we were seeing very little of each other, because I was fearful that the break might somehow upset the emotional equilibrium I'd regained after passing through my crisis. I didn't feel I had the energy to cope with being unsettled again, even though I received almost no emotional support from the boyfriend who was not interested in having his carefree life weighed down by my problems.

However, the conviction and urging of the Holy Spirit was heavy on me:

God's will is for you to be holy, so stay away from all sexual sin. Then each of you will control his own body and live in holiness and honour— not in lustful passion like the pagans who do not know God and his ways. (1 Thessalonians 4:3-5 NLT)

It took three months for me to obey God, and what helped the decision was that I wanted to attend an evening service at a particular charismatic church in Melbourne where I felt I would best fit in. Up until then, I had been attending church on Sunday mornings which was easy to keep secret from friends and family as they thought I was out shopping, but changing to the Sunday evenings would complicate things with the boyfriend. I still hadn't told anyone that I had become a Christian. I was faced with the decision of either having to lie about where I was going on Sunday nights or ending the relationship. I decided to make the break and prayed to God that He would strengthen me and keep my emotions balanced.

I remember very clearly the day I ended the relationship. Directly after, I prayed to God repenting of my sins. I was immediately overwhelmed with a feeling of freedom and elation. I was at perfect peace and I knew the Holy Spirit was pleased. Not once did I look back, feel sad or regret the break; I only regretted that I had not obeyed God sooner and trusted Him to uphold me.

MY FAVOURITE CHURCH

I had been told about powerful charismatic services at a church in East Brunswick called Our Lady Help of Christians. I went along to this church one Sunday evening to see for myself. I arrived early and was surprised by how many other people were there half an hour before the service was due to start. Most had already reserved 'their seat' with a cushion and handbag. I immediately felt more at home in this church than at St Augustine's because there were more people my age and whose backgrounds I could identify with.

The services at this church were something special. The

worship was anointed and soothing, the beautiful stained glass windows reflected coloured lights onto the walls as the sun went down, and the church was candle lit. More importantly, the priest, Father Victor, welcomed in the presence of the Holy Spirit so powerfully.

Two things I miss about the Catholic Charismatic services, now that I move in Pentecostal church circles, are the time and honour they gave at the start of each service to welcome in the presence of the Holy Spirit, releasing Him to start healing and touching lives as people sat through the service. It makes such a difference. Also, usually, straight after worship, the priest would have us sit silently in the presence of the Lord, waiting on Him to move. Sometimes, the whole church would hold hands with the people beside them while we waited. As we sat, the presence of the Holy Spirit became stronger and hovered over us. Many cried, some were delivered, and every now and then the priest would have a word of knowledge about someone with a particular problem that the Lord was healing at that moment. We would sit this way anywhere from ten minutes to half an hour. This was my favourite part of the service. When I first came into Pentecostal services, I was frustrated by the constant noise of worship and speaking and wondered when time would be made to let God move in response to all of the prayer and worship. I really believe this is something very important that's missing in the services and prayer meetings I attend in Pentecostal churches.

Over the course of the next few months, I attended many conferences, mostly on healing, and there were many visiting priests and lay ministers from around the world who ministered in the church. I enjoyed learning from the different speakers and watching and receiving from their individual ministry styles, all the while receiving more and more healing for layers of small issues that most people accumulate through life, especially when they haven't known Jesus.

Many of the people within the congregation also had ministries within the church. Some focused on emotional healing, some of physical healing, some had the gift of the discernment of spirits and others prophesied, just as it says in the Bible:

There are different kinds of gifts, but the same Spirit distributes them. There are different kinds of service, but the same Lord. There are different kinds of working, but in all of them and in everyone it is the same God at work.

Now to each one the manifestation of the Spirit is given for the common good. To one there is given through the Spirit a message of wisdom, to another a message of knowledge by means of the same Spirit, to another faith by the same Spirit, to another gifts of healing by that one Spirit, to another miraculous powers, to another prophecy, to another distinguishing between spirits, to another speaking in different kinds of tongues, and to still another the interpretation of tongues. All these are the work of one and the same Spirit, and he distributes them to each one, just as he determines. (1 Corinthians 12:4-11)

A friend told me about a couple who had a ministry of inner healing and had helped him by praying with him through issues he had with his father. I made a time to see them. They prayed with me and asked if I'd ever prayed to break soul ties. I didn't know what this was, so they explained.

There can be healthy and unhealthy soul ties between people. Soul ties can be sexual and non-sexual. Examples of healthy soul ties are parents' bonds with their children, relationships amongst family members, close friends and the sexual relationship between husband and wife. Ungodly or spiritually unhealthy soul ties are those where 'normal' relationships with family, friends or people are corrupted by abuse, fear, control, obsession, lust or dependency, or where there has been sexual relationship outside of marriage. Ungodly soul ties provide open doors to unclean spirits.

The Bible is clear that people's souls knit together through marriage and sexual relationship (Ephesians 5:31):

For this reason a man will leave his father and mother and be united to his wife, and the two will become one flesh.

The Bible also warns against ungodly sexual soul ties in 1 Corinthians 6:16:

Do you not know that your bodies are members of Christ himself? Shall I then take the members of Christ and unite them with a prostitute? Never! Do you not know that he who unites himself with a prostitute is one with her in body? For it is said, "The two will become one flesh."

If a person has sexual relationships outside marriage, he or she potentially opens spiritual doors to whatever spiritual baggage the sexual partner is carrying.

The couple led me through a prayer to repent and cut myself off spiritually from previous partners. In learning about soul ties and praying to clear them, I had a revelation that the soul tie I had formed with Stephen years before had an influence on me during my crisis, particularly with the irrational suicidal obsession. Stephen had been mentally ill for a number of years with bi-polar disorder or schizophrenia, and his ups and downs echoed in my life years after we had separated. However, I realised that this tie had broken off me when Stephen died. Soul ties can be broken when a person dies, which is why a person is free to marry again after a marriage partner dies. Soul ties can also be broken through prayer. I have included a prayer to break soul ties at the end of the book for anyone who needs to do the same.

Spring cleaning my life of things I hadn't realised are New Age

Another topic I read a lot about and needed to do a lot of repenting and praying about in the early days of my Christian life was my involvement in the New Age. The more I read, the more I recognised how many New Age practices I had dabbled in, mostly unwittingly, over the years.

Derek Prince's books taught me more than any other books about areas I needed to cut from my life, which I hadn't realised were of the New Age and which posed open doors to demonic spirits. The first discovery was that yoga is unacceptable to God and is a New Age practice. I had practised yoga for about seven years and really enjoyed it. I realised that there was a Hindu philosophy behind it that some people chose to delve into, but I wasn't interested in that and I thought I was fine just going along to do the stretches.

Several of Prince's books detail his background in yoga before he was saved. At one stage, Prince aspired to become a yogi, a spiritual master. On the night Derek Prince was saved, in a tent in the desert while he was serving in the army, the power of God came down on him and he believed that during his remarkable salvation experience he was delivered from the spirit of yoga.[17]

When I read this, it took a little while to digest and accept the information and reflect over what it was we did in yoga classes. The more I thought about it, the more the Holy Spirit seemed to bring to mind aspects of yoga poses and practices that were based on Eastern spirituality, which I hadn't been aware of before. For instance, a standard pose and routine of movements in a yoga class is called 'Salute to the Sun.' Whether a person realises it or not, believes in a sun god or not, he or she is being led through worship of a false god. Spiritual laws are similar to man-made laws: ignorance of the law or spiritual forces is no defence against the law or spiritual forces. Demonic forces will look for the smallest opportunity or legal right to come into your life. This legal right isn't nullified until you repent of your sins, which is hard to do if you aren't aware you're sinning or don't accept that something you're doing is incompatible with Christianity and abhorrent to God. Many other names of poses within yoga also honour Hindu gods and symbolise stories about them and lessons learnt through Hindu lore.

Another standard practice within a yoga class is 'relaxation time' at the end of the session. Relaxation time in this context is guided meditation. Meditation is another New Age practice which stems from Eastern philosophy and is intrinsically linked to Eastern religions, particularly Buddhism and Hinduism. New Age meditation is different to what Christians call meditation. Christian meditation involves focusing on Scripture and filling your mind with God's Word and promises. In contrast, the aim of New Age meditation is to clear or blank the mind so it can 'become one' with the universe, free from all distractions and earthly pettiness. The yoga teacher guides the class through a series of visualisation exercises, such as focusing with the mind's eye on an imagined light a metre above the head, with the aim having an out of body experience. It's actually quite difficult to have an out of body experience at will, so yogis and Buddhists spend years trying to master this ability, all the while opening themselves to more demonic influences. Any time the body or mind is left an empty vessel or a person is not in control of their body and will, such as when someone is drunk or drugged to the point of unconsciousness, or when a person is fully anaesthetized in an operation, they are vulnerable to the demonic.

After seven years of attending yoga classes, I gave them up as soon as I realised and accepted that there was a problem with yoga. There are so many other forms of exercise to choose from that it simply was not worth the spiritual risk continuing. I had made the decision to obey God no matter what, and I was sticking to that. If something you're involved in is spiritually questionable, it's always best to stay on the safe side where God is concerned. I wanted a clean slate before God so that nothing would hinder the blessing or abundant life and total restoration I was determined to claim.

CURSED OBJECTS

Through reading more of Derek Prince's books and teachings, I also came to learn about cursed objects and how they can attract and be a home to demonic spirits. Prince writes about some beautiful silk embroidered dragons he had framed and hanging on the wall which his grandfather had given him. In seeking God for an answer about what was blocking him from having financial abundance, God kept showing him the pictures of the dragons. Prince had treasured the gifts from his grandfather and it took him time to accept and obey God's prompting to destroy them. The dragon is a symbol of the devil. When Prince did destroy the pictures, he immediately experienced a supernatural inflow of finances.

I mulled over this testimony for some time. I had many African masks, Indian statues and Indonesian puppets in my home as decorative objects. I kept looking at them wondering if they really could be homes for demonic spirits. I was also aware of the scripture: *'You shall not make for yourself an idol in the form of anything in heaven above or on the earth beneath or in the waters below. You shall not bow down to them or worship them.'* (Exodus 20:4-5)

One morning, I woke and found that the face of an Indonesian shadow puppet I had in my bathroom was so ugly and ghoulish, that on a whim I picked it up, snapped it over my knee and said, 'Today, you're going!' I then threw the broken pieces in the bin.

After destroying the puppet, I was woken in the middle of the night by three heavy punches on the pillow next to my head. I also heard violent breathing close to my ear. I understood that this was the demonic spirit that had been released from the puppet. Shaken, I thought to myself, 'Oh, it is real!' The next day, I took the rest of my masks and statues, outside and destroyed them with an axe. This time I prayed over the statues, binding and rebuking any spirits that might have been housed in them. There was a discernible difference in the atmosphere of my home after clearing these things out. How many people today have decorative statues of Buddha in their home or garden without realising what they could house?

As well as masks and statues that represented or symbolised false gods, Prince also wrote about other possessions that can attract demonic spirits. I set about doing a major spring clean of books and movies that I felt contained language or content that isn't acceptable to God. I also threw out trinkets and jewellery such as crystals that were sold as healing crystals. Thousands of dollars' worth of New Age books and other objects were thrown out. It wasn't easy doing this, and I had to battle the thought that I could sell all of these things, but I knew that if I did that I would be passing on a curse to others. Once all of these cursed objects were done away with, I did have a deep peace about it and haven't regretted or looked back since:

> *Many who became believers confessed their sinful practices. A number of them who had been practicing sorcery brought their incantation books and burned them at a public bonfire. The value of the books was several million dollars.* (Acts 19:18 NLT)

There are many other New Age practices that I tried over the years. So that I don't break the flow of my testimony by getting too bogged down in going through all of the therapies, I have included a section later in book in which I discuss many of these other modalities and I explain why they pose spiritual problems.

MOVING ON

I eventually informed my parents that I had become a Christian, although I did not explain what I had been through. My father was delighted. My mother, who wasn't a Christian at the time, was baffled and wondered what had happened to me and worried that I had joined a cult.

I kept my Christianity private at the school where I taught as everyone had always known me as an outspoken atheist. My own salvation and understanding of the Bible and God was all too new and private at that point for me to have launched out and attempted to share my experience with many people. While the school I had taught at for eleven years was non-denominational and open to all faiths, its flavour was anti-Christian. I wasn't ready to brave the questions and reactions of the school community by letting them know I had become a radical Christian overnight. I started to desire and pray for a big change in my life. Initially, I wanted to shift to teaching in a Christian school where I wouldn't feel a need to hide my new faith. I also wanted to 'start again' and had this scripture on my mind, 'Leave your country, your people and your father's household and go to the land I will show you.' (Genesis 12:1) More than this, I also wanted to serve God. I had no idea how I might do this, but after more than 17 years as a high school English teacher, I was ready for a change. I started praying for the change in earnest, but didn't get any ideas back from God. I thought that I would like to move to Sydney and teach in a beautiful girls' school I had seen that overlooked Sydney Harbour, so I started to pray for this.

In the meantime, a friend at church mentioned her struggle in choosing between her Catholic background and the leading she felt to change to a Pentecostal church. I was so new and green to church and religious politics that I had very little idea of what the problem was in making the shift. They all believed in Jesus as the only Lord and read the same Bible, didn't they? I had a vague understanding that some people objected to Catholicism because of the statues in the churches, prayers to Mary and worship of the Catholic Saints. I did wonder about the scriptures that mentioned idol worship, such as, 'Do not turn to idols or make for yourselves any gods of cast metal: I am the Lord your God' (Leviticus 19:4), but I thought that these statues were just reminders of what Jesus had done and of Christian stories. I didn't see people worshipping the statues themselves and I had not heard anyone lead a prayer to Mary in a Charismatic service.

My friend knew that I was interested in healing and asked me if I would like to come along in a few weeks to see John Mellor minister in a Pentecostal church in the outer suburbs of Melbourne. I had never heard of John Mellor. My friend told me about the miracles she had witnessed the last time John ministered at this church. She had witnessed a young man who had been deaf from birth receiving his hearing, and listening to a piano being played and a guitar being strummed for the first time in his life. I decided to go along.

Before going along to John's meeting, I looked up his website and was excited to see so many outstanding testimonies of people healed of all sorts of conditions that are medically impossible to heal.[18]

MEETING JOHN

I went along to John's healing meeting which was in a large church on the outskirts of Melbourne. I was amazed to witness so many people being instantly healed of all sorts of conditions. By this stage, I had attended many healing meetings with other ministers, but this was the first time I had been to a healing meeting where the minister prayed for more than a few seconds for each person and actually waited to see if the person was feeling better. With John's ministry, roughly 80% of the people he prayed for testified on the spot that they could no longer feel any symptoms of their condition.

In the meeting, a time came when everyone who wanted prayer was welcome to come and queue at the front. I went up. As I stood in the line and John came closer, about four or five people away, I could feel the anointing of God radiate from him and I found it difficult to remain standing as my head went woozy and my legs wanted to give way. When it was my turn to be prayed for, I was overwhelmed by the presence of God. I felt something rise up from my stomach and leave through my throat and then I fell on the floor. Obviously, some sort of spirit left me, though I'm not exactly sure what it was. John's healing anointing was and still is the most powerful I've experienced through any healing evangelist.

To cut a long story short, over the next six months, John ministered often in Melbourne churches not too far from where I lived. I attended many of these meetings and so he got to know me by sight and we had a few brief conversations.

Towards the end of 2007, God prompted me through a vision to hurry up and send unsolicited teaching applications to Christian schools in Sydney and the Sunshine Coast in Queensland. My desire was to teach at the girls' school I'd seen overlooking Sydney Harbour, but I also sent three applications to Christian schools I knew of on the Sunshine Coast. I had lived on the Sunshine Coast many years before, and I had holidayed there for years so I knew a few people up there and some teachers who had also made the shift north. I prayed over my applications and asked God to bless whichever application and school He wanted me to go to. I sent the applications off by email one afternoon.

The very next morning when I arrived in my office, I received a phone call from a school on the Sunshine Coast. One of their English teachers had handed in his resignation that morning and they had received the unsolicited email application from me. I was invited to attend an interview in two weeks' time. I knew in my spirit that I had the job there if I wanted it, but I was still praying for a Sydney application to be accepted.

In the two weeks of waiting to go up to the Sunshine Coast for the interview, John was conducting a three-day teaching seminar in Melbourne. Unusually, I could attend much of the seminar during the day because my students were all sitting final year exams and I was free to be away from school. Also speaking at the seminar was John's pastor, Dr Chas Gullo, who has a particular ministry focus on building strong families and marriages. This is the only time to date that John has travelled and ministered with Chas. I knew Chas was the senior pastor of a school that was close to the school where I would be attending the interview. I approached Chas to ask him questions about the school. He in turn asked lots of questions about me, which I found a little odd. However, at the end of the seminar, the reason for his inquisition became clear when he asked me if I'd like to meet up with John when I went up for my interview.

I went up to the Sunshine Coast and attended the interview. I was offered the teaching job. I met up with John for dinner. In January 2008, I moved up to the Sunshine Coast. It was a step of faith and obedience for me to make the shift. I was leaving a school I had been very comfortable in for 11 years and where I held a senior position that paid very well. I was taking a substantial pay cut and demotion in moving to the school on the Sunshine Coast, but I had made the decision to obey God and He was clearly guiding me to make the move.

The day after all of my furniture had arrived on the Sunshine Coast, a message came through on my mobile phone voicemail. Strangely, the message was a week old and it was from the Sydney girls' school on the Harbour that I had been praying for. One of their English teachers had resigned and they wanted to know if I could attend an urgent interview. I realised that if the message had come through to me on the day it was sent, I would still have been in Melbourne and perhaps could have been tempted to quickly jump ship and direct the delivery truck to Sydney. God's hand and will for me to be on the Sunshine Coast was underlined yet again.

At the same time as my move to Queensland, John was basing himself back in Australia after ten years of itinerant international ministry. After being on the road and having no home or car of his own for a decade, God told him to focus on ministering mainly in Australia. He moved seven minutes down the road from where I was living. Of course he was away ministering most weekends, but when back at home during the week he would visit me in the evening around dinner time. I invited him to have dinner with me and, rather like a stray cat, he would be back the next night around dinner time and I'd feed him again. I think John married me because he enjoys my cooking!

Several months into our relationship, John started talking of marriage. This was too soon for me as I wasn't sure that I wanted to be married. There was one morning when John had come back from a weekend of ministry and he came over to have breakfast with me before I went to work. It had been raining very heavily for at least 24 hours. As I was getting ready to leave for work he said, 'I wish you had the day off so that we could go to the movies. If we were married I'd get to see you all the time.'

I replied, 'If God wants us to marry, then He's going to need to send me a pretty big sign.'

'What sort of sign?' John asked.

I joked, 'If God wants us to marry, he'll flood my school and I can come home and we can go to the movies!'

I drove off to school.

As I approached the school gates, I could see staff standing in the rain with trousers rolled up to their knees waving cars away. During the night, the trickle of a creek that ran through the school grounds had become blocked with debris and the flow was redirected along the walking paths straight into the school. The school was flooded under a foot of water! A science teacher had caught a fish in the locker hall and another staff member had his surfboard out. All of the students were sent home and once they were gone, all staff went home.

John and I ended up going to the movies.

At the end of the year we were married. Since then, we have travelled and ministered together constantly, throughout Australia and overseas.

*Practices you might
not be aware involve
the New Age*

The idols speak deceit, diviners see visions that lie; they tell dreams that are false, they give comfort in vain. Therefore the people wander like sheep oppressed for lack of a shepherd.

Zechariah 10:2

When my husband, John, is invited to present healing seminars as part of our ministry in churches, he often invites me to share my testimony and talk about a few of my New Age experiences as part of our teaching on hindrances to healing. However, in this section, I will share some more of my experiences and discuss a number of other New Age practices that I am often asked about at our meetings. There is a lot for Christians to learn about the New Age and how and why its popularity is spreading widely. It's also important to realise that the New Age constantly changes its face and the names of its therapies and modalities.

In my case, I turned to the New Age because of the marketing. I didn't fully realise that what I was looking into was the New Age and that's the case for many other people today. New Age practitioners invest a lot of money in advertising, often taking out whole A4 or A3-sized advertisements in colourful monthly health magazines that are free for the public to take outside health food shops and businesses promoting alternative lifestyles. These New Age advertisements make huge promises about what can be accomplished through their methods, such as curing any disease, regrowing body parts, reversing ageing, reprogramming DNA, attaining the life of your dreams with the perfect partner, unlimited wealth and an ideal career.

Another aspect of the New Age that contributes to blinding people to its spiritual dangers and unsubstantiated claims is the way it has aligned itself with healthy living. It is a great shame that most health food shops have become centres that promote New Age practices and beliefs, advertising everything from yoga classes, meditation retreats, Ayurvedic Medicine and Traditional Chinese Medicine, homeopathy and crystals, creating the impression by association that New Age practices are healthy and natural.

There are also many charismatic New Age practitioners whose personalities create a following. The assumption is that if this leader - who looks the epitome of health and happiness - represents our goal, then if we follow what they teach, we too will be transformed. Many people are vulnerable to the persuasion of other people. We see this in the Christian culture too. Many people look to my husband, John, with his healing gift, as if he holds all of the answers to their problems.

It is also important to be aware that many people are drawn to become practitioners of New Age modalities because they are looking for a lifestyle change. Because there are no regulations surrounding alternative health practices, it is possible to set up a business instantly. The training for these therapies is not formal or long, in most cases. Often a weekend intensive or a 12-week course is enough to train people to practice a modality. From my experience, many people in the New Age charge more than it costs to see a medical doctor, so it is a highly lucrative industry, particularly for those who are charismatic.

John and I constantly have people come to our healing meetings who practise New Age therapies and are sick. They are often powerfully touched and healed by God, and yet they do not receive Jesus as Lord. The obstacle to them following Jesus is that they realise that they would have to give up their form of income and they are usually not willing to do that. We have seen this scenario so many times. Reiki healers have come to our meetings and been healed of conditions such as Multiple Sclerosis, blindness and a broken leg and yet they shy away from receiving Jesus. It's like the story in Acts 16:16-19, where Paul and Silas deliver a fortune teller of a demonic spirit:

One day as we were going down to the place of prayer,

we met a demon-possessed slave girl. She was a fortune-teller who earned a lot of money for her masters. She followed Paul and the rest of us, shouting, "These men are servants of the Most High God, and they have come to tell you how to be saved." This went on day after day until Paul got so exasperated that he turned and said to the demon within her, "I command you in the name of Jesus Christ to come out of her." And instantly it left her. Her masters' hopes of wealth were now shattered, so they grabbed Paul and Silas and dragged them before the authorities at the marketplace.' (NLT)

Earlier in my book, I discussed the spiritual problems with yoga, meditation, The Reconnection, Quantum Touch and Theta Healing. In this section, I discuss some of the most common New Age modalities, as well as some stranger therapies I tried, just to provide a fuller awareness of what is on offer. Many readers will be surprised to find a number of therapies listed that have now become a familiar adjunct to mainstream medicine and physical therapies, but they actually involve spiritual aspects or scientific quackery, and are not taught in medical school.

The following discussion of therapies is by no means definitive. Every month new therapies are invented and launched as the latest and greatest revelation of long lost ancient keys to healing, achieving your dreams and higher consciousness; but they are in fact a repackaged mix of what already exists, renamed and trademarked by a marketing savvy New Age entrepreneur.

I would like to reiterate a point I made earlier: although there may be some positives and truths in some of these therapies, there are also many false claims and spiritual aspects mixed in which can be problematic, either because they pose an open spiritual door to the demonic or because people ignore mainstream western medicine to follow treatments that are marketed as natural and less damaging to our health. Also, whenever you submit to someone for a treatment, you give honour to them, their knowledge, experiences and beliefs, regardless of whether or not you are aware of the spiritual philosophies behind their beliefs. The devil doesn't play fair, and many people can unwittingly expose themselves to the demonic through New Age therapies and therapists.

My knowledge in writing about these therapies comes from a mixture of my own personal experiences, as well as from reading many books and websites on these therapies. I threw out all of my New Age books when I became a Christian so I do not reference these, but in the end references, I list the websites from which I quote information in the following summaries. Please be aware that websites are constantly changing and being updated, so the version of what you find in the future may vary from the information I found at the time of writing this book.

There are also many excellent Christian websites that provide information about the spiritual dangers of New Age practices; many of these are compiled by former New Age practitioners who have converted to Christianity. These websites can be found by entering an internet search under a subject such as 'Christian view of New Age.'

One particular handbook I recommend and have drawn information from extensively is *Alternative Medicine: The Options, The Claims, The Evidence, How to Choose Wisely,* by Donal O'Mathuna and Walt Larimore, who are members of the Christian Medical Association.[19] In this handbook, the writers assess many forms of complementary and alternative medicine and report on whether or not the science these therapies put forward is clinically verifiable, as well as pointing out quack treatments and the spiritual dangers associated with many therapies.

Another highly recommended and very interesting read and source of information on the New Age is a secular report and summary of Complementary and Alternative Medicine produced by the *British Parliamentary Commission into Alternative Medicine in 1999-2000*. The report considers the reasons why people seek alternative medicine, which is often related to lack of satisfaction, time, attention and availability of help from mainstream doctors. Interestingly, the report concludes that while scientific evidence is lacking to demonstrate that most alternative therapies do little if anything to help heal the sick in any real terms, the patient's perceived level of satisfaction with the time and level of concern shown by alternative therapists has value and these therapies filled a gap in health care that mainstream medicine is currently unable to satisfy.[20]

The following is a brief summary of other forms of New Age therapy and medicine, most of which I have tried or am often asked about in our healing seminars when I share my testimony. I also mention a few key figures within the New Age who have huge followings around the world.

Traditional Chinese Medicine

Traditional Chinese Medicine (TCM) covers a broad range of practices based on the ancient Chinese Taoist spiritual philosophy of chi: the invisible life force energy thought to flow through all living things. Its therapies include herbal medicine, acupuncture, exercise (qigong), massage and dietary therapy.[21] TCM does not diagnose or treat illness using knowledge of the anatomy or the scientific basis of conventional modern western medicine. Instead, it uses mystical principles of yin and yang – which is the balance of the flow of chi throughout the body and organs. TCM believes that if there's sickness in the body, then there's a blockage in the flow and harmony of chi, and so one or more therapies are recommended to deal with the blockage and restore the flow of chi and health to the body.

Scientific evidence proving that the range of TCM treatments has a positive effect on health is scarce and varies for each therapy, some of which I will discuss in more detail. There are many common sense approaches and principles for health in TCM, such as eating a balanced, healthy diet, exercising and reducing stress. However, many TCM therapies are not clinically verified and people seeking diagnosis of disease through TCM run the risk of not having their illness properly diagnosed or treated, when safe and effective conventional medicines and therapies are available.

Some herbs commonly used within TCM have been shown to be effective, but many substances that go into TCM herbal mixes have not been tested and are included for spiritual reasons, such as parts of animals, which can be toxic. Additionally, anyone seeking TCM is invariably exposed to the Taoist religious and philosophical beliefs, thereby opening them to the demonic realm.

Acupuncture

Acupuncture and acupressure are based on Taoist religious and philosophical principles. From a Christian standpoint, they are occultic. Acupuncture and acupressure apply stimulation to points on the body to stimulate the flow of cosmic life-energy through channels in the body practitioners call 'meridians'. These meridians are invisible and do not physically exist, they are a spiritual concept. It's believed that when there is an imbalance in the flow of life-energy, disease comes. Therapists believe that acupuncture and acupressure can unblock the imbalance. This life-energy is called 'chi' in Chinese, 'ki' in

Japanese and 'prana' in Hindi.

Many scientific studies have examined the efficacy of acupuncture and found that it produces little measurable result outside placebo effect. Placebo effect can be attributed for up to 30% of a person's perceived change of symptoms. There are also possible risks of infection and nerve damage through the use of needle acupuncture.

The spiritual risk with acupuncture is that by consenting to treatment, a patient gives honour to the traditional Eastern philosophies and religious beliefs that underpin the practice. These beliefs are not compatible with Christianity because they ultimately worship false gods and provide an open door to demonic spirits.

Reflexology

Reflexology is an offshoot of acupressure, involving foot or hand massage. Reflexologists believe that sections of the hand and feet correlate through the nervous system to specific organs in the body. They believe that when there is illness in the body, there is a blockage in the life force energies of the body, and that massage of the hands or feet can break up crystalline deposits causing the blockage, restoring the flow of energy and health. Medically and anatomically, reflexology's claims are laughable. A problem with reflexology is that people might just think they are getting a thorough foot massage, but they are potentially at spiritual risk, being exposed to New Age Eastern philosophies and possible energy channelling or use of spirit guides by the practitioner.

Ayurvedic Medicine

In most health food shops these days, there is a growing array of potions, teas and creams that are grouped in an Ayurvedic section. Ayurvedic medicine is the Hindu equivalent of Traditional Chinese Medicine. It is said to originate from revelations from the Hindu gods and therefore from the Christian viewpoint it is occultic and spiritually dangerous, stemming from a false religion. Ayurvedic medicine aims to treat not only physical complaints, but also mental and spiritual issues. It is not based on traditional western medicine and knowledge of the anatomy, but rather on the Hindu view of the anatomy which involves belief in 'chakras', which are thought to be spiritual centres throughout the body, and a spiritual energy flow through the body Hindus call 'prana', the Hindu equivalent of the Chinese 'chi'. Practitioners aim to regulate the energy flow through the body by mastering consciousness through practices such as yoga, meditation and diet to affect the body.

While many Ayurvedic creams and potions contain everyday ingredients you would find elsewhere on health food shelves and in supermarkets, the spiritual basis for the products means that it is best to avoid them.

Dr Deepak Chopra

There are many charismatic leaders and prolific writers within the New Age who have huge followings around the world and are often befriended by celebrities who help to promote their beliefs. Deepak Chopra is one of the best known figures in the New Age. His background is interesting because he trained in western medicine in America, but gave that up to follow Ayruvedic medicine. Below I quote a critic of Chopra because the assessment reinforces many points I have made about how the New Age uses pseudo-scientific and psychological terms. It is important to be aware that having a background in science and western medicine does not exclude a person from being open to the spiritual, occultic and New Age. Chopra refers to the shortcomings of science and medicine as reasons why he chose to investigate consciousness and the spiritual:

Deepak Chopra is an Indian-born, American physician and writer. Chopra has taught at the medical schools of Tufts University, Boston University and Harvard University. He became Chief of Staff at the New England Memorial Hospital (NEMH) in Massachusetts before establishing a private practice. In 1985, Chopra met Maharishi Mahesh Yogi, who invited him to study Ayurveda. Chopra left his position at the NEMH and became the founding president of the American Association of Ayurvedic Medicine, and was later named medical director of the Maharishi Ayurveda Health Center.

In 1996, Chopra and neurologist David Simon founded the Chopra Center for Wellbeing, which incorporated Ayurveda in its regimen, and was located in La Jolla, California. The University of California, San Diego, School of Medicine and American Medical Association have granted continuing medical education credits for some programs offered to physicians at the Chopra Center. In 2002, Chopra and Simon relocated the Chopra Center to the grounds of La Costa Resort and Spa in Carlsbad, California. In 2009, Chopra established the Chopra Foundation to advance the cause of mind/body spiritual healing, education, and research through fundraising for selected projects.

According to a 2008 article in <u>Time</u> magazine, Chopra is "a magnet for criticism", primarily from those involved in science and medicine. Some critics say that Chopra creates a false sense of hope in sick individuals which may keep them away from effective medical care. The Time article summarized Chopra's reception and popularity thus: "Of all the Asian gurus..., Chopra has arguably been the most successful at erasing apparent differences between East and West by packaging Eastern mystique in credible Western garb. ...His *quest to construct a pleasing and seamless model of the universe tends to jump to easy conclusions and to spackle over problematic gaps and inconsistencies in the ideas he presents — is obvious to all but his most starry-eyed fans..."*

In 1998, Chopra was awarded the satirical Ig Nobel Prize in physics for "his unique interpretation of quantum physics as it applies to life, liberty, and the pursuit of economic happiness." According to the book Skeptics Dictionary, Chopra's "mind-body claims get even murkier as he tries to connect Ayurveda with quantum physics." Chopra also participated in the Channel 4 (UK) documentary The Enemies of Reason, *where, when interviewed by scientist Richard Dawkins, he admitted that the term "quantum theory" was being used as a metaphor and that it has little to do with the actual quantum theory in physics.*

In March 2010, Chopra and Jean Houston debated Sam Harris and Michael Shermer at Caltech on the question "Does God Have a Future?" Shermer and Harris criticized Chopra's use of scientific terminology to expound unrelated spiritual concepts. Shermer has said that Chopra is "the very definition of what we mean by pseudoscience".

In April 2010, Hindu American Foundation co-founder Aseem Shukla, on a Washington Post-sponsored blog on faith and religion, criticized Chopra for suggesting that yoga did not have origins in Hinduism but is an older Indian spiritual tradition which predated Hinduism.[73] Later on, Chopra explained yoga as rooted in "consciousness alone" which is a universal, non-sectarian eternal wisdom of life expounded by Vedic rishis long before historic Hinduism ever arose. He further accused Aseem Shukla of having a "fundamentalist agenda". Dr. Shukla in a rejoinder titled "Dr. Chopra: Honor thy heritage" termed Deepak Chopra as an exponent of the art of

"How to Deconstruct, Repackage and Sell Hindu Philosophy Without Calling it Hindu!" [22]

Louise Hay

Louise Hay is another prominent New Age/self-help guru whose books *You Can Heal Your Life* and *Heal Your Body* are among the best-selling New Age books that can be found in any secular bookshop. Hay is best known for her teachings about positive thinking and affirmations. Many of the philosophies Hay teaches, such as the importance of guarding against resentment and negative thoughts and feelings for a healthy, happy life, are common sense truths, but the danger with her teachings is that her New Age beliefs about the universe, Law of Attraction and God being vague 'universal love' are so subtly entwined in her language that it requires spiritual discernment to detect. Many people, particularly women, subscribe to receiving Hays' daily positive affirmations by email or Facebook, unaware that they are being exposed to New Age philosophies and simply embracing them as harmless positivity.[23]

Hay joined and trained in the cult group, Religious Science, also known as Science of Mind, in the 1970s, as well as studying Transcendental Meditation with the Maharishi Yogi. Religious Science considers itself a blend of science, religion and philosophy and makes references to Jesus Christ, the Bible and Buddha in its teachings. Religious Science founder, Ernest Holmes' philosophy is that:

...all beings are expressions of and part of Infinite Intelligence, also known as Spirit, Christ Consciousness, or God. It teaches that, because God is all there is in the universe (not just present in Heaven, or in assigned deities, as believed by traditional teachings), Its power can be used by all humans to the extent that they recognize and align themselves with Its

presence. Ernest Holmes said "God is not ... a person, but a Universal Presence... already in our own soul, already operating through our own consciousness.'

RS/SOM teaches that people can achieve more fulfilling lives through the practice called Spiritual Mind Treatment (Treatment), or Affirmative Prayer. Spiritual Mind Treatment is a step-by-step process, in which one states the desired outcome as if it has already happened. In that way, it differs from traditional prayer, since it does not ask an entity separate from itself to act. It declares human partnership with Infinite Intelligence to achieve success.[24]

Louise Hay has her own publishing company, Hay House, and publishes books by Deepak Chopra and also the teachings of Abraham by Esther Hicks, amongst other New Age teachers.

New Age practices which involve the laying on of hands or channelling of energy for healing

The following practices can look very much like Christian laying on of hands for healing, but they call on and use a spiritual source of healing, such as the energy of the universe and angel or spirit guides, which is expressly forbidden and warned against in the Bible:

- Reiki
- Pranic Healing
- Quantum Touch
- Therapeutic Touch
- Polarity Therapy
- Chakra balancing
- Vibrational Healing

There are many more forms of New Age energy healing and hands-on healing than listed above; practitioners constantly invent new names for modalities which are essentially the same as those listed.

Hypnotherapy

Hypnotherapy is one of the practices I'm often asked about. These days, many people complete a series of eight weekend intensive courses and set themselves up as hypnotherapists who claim to be able to cure depression, low self-esteem, phobias and addictions - such as smoking - instantly. I've met a number of these hypnotherapists at our healing meetings. The irony is that they come to our meetings for prayer for issues that they claim to be able to 'cure' themselves with hypnotherapy. Very often in the New Age, people looking for healing for themselves take part in courses hoping to be healed, and then become practitioners - while they are still on the journey to healing themselves.

Exactly how hypnotherapy works is medically unknown. Anton Mesmer, a hypnotist and psychic, is considered the modern founder of the technique. Hypnosis involves the deliberate inducement of a willing patient to a state of trance and heightened suggestibility. In this state, a person's consciousness is thought to be flexible and open to manipulation.[25]

The spiritual concern with hypnotherapy is that in this state of submission of will to the hypnotherapist, the patient could be potentially opening him or herself up to demonic forces, especially to whatever spiritual weaknesses may exist in the hypnotherapist's life.

Martial Arts (judo, karate, tai chi, tae kwon do, etc.)

There are two schools of Christian thought regarding whether or not forms of martial arts are spiritually suspect. One side argues that some forms of martial arts, such as judo, were developed purely for self-defence. However, others argue that, similar to yoga, you cannot separate the Eastern philosophies and religious concepts behind the practices from the physical poses. The martial arts emphasise the control of mind and body for self-defence and, very often, spiritual enlightenment. Many modes of martial arts warm up with meditation practices that seek to unify mind, spirit and body which they believe help to regulate the flow of life force energy or chi and help to attain a state of 'oneness' with the universe.

Tai chi is considered by the Chinese to be an 'internal' martial art. It's common to observe groups of people, particularly the elderly, performing tai chi in public gardens and at the beach, and it looks like an innocuous form of exercise; however, it is highly spiritual in purpose. The reason that these groups prefer to practise outside is because they believe they are drawing on the energy of the universe more strongly by having their feet on bare earth. Again, as with me and yoga, many people attend martial arts classes who are interested only in the physical exercise, but they are unwittingly exposed to the underlying philosophies and therefore potentially open spiritual doors to the demonic.

Muscle Testing

Muscle testing, also called Applied Kinesiology and Touch for Health, is widely used in chiropractic and Chinese acupuncture therapy. It involves the diagnosis of a physical problem by testing the supposed weakness of muscles which are believed to be related to corresponding organs. It's thought that weak muscles indicate weak 'energy' in the related organs, producing a susceptibility to disease.

One technique within muscle testing is called the 'challenge technique' where a substance that is suspected of causing harm to the body, such as wheat or dairy products, is held in one hand and the therapist pushes down on the patient's other arm which is raised at shoulder height to assess whether the substance has a weakening effect on the body. If the arm goes down, then it is diagnosed that the patient is intolerant to that substance and requires treatment to heal the sensitivity. There are many variations of this technique. Practitioners explain that the technique works because the cells in the body intrinsically know the answer to all questions in the universe. Chiropractors commonly use this technique to 'prove' to the patient that a misalignment is causing a subsequent weakness in the associated limb and therefore requires manipulation to correct it.

Furthermore, muscle testing often involves the use and manipulation of 'universal energies,' as well as acupressure and its associated meridian tracing to treat or heal the patient by unblocking supposedly congested energy pathways in the body. This manipulation of invisible energies makes it potentially occultic through the channelling of or calling on 'energies' - or any spirit that will answer the call. Muscle testing is scientifically unsubstantiated.

I encountered the use of muscle testing in many New Age modalities as well as therapies such as chiropractic. One particular therapy I tried in the hope of dealing with minor allergies relied heavily on muscle testing to both diagnose and heal allergies. Only a few years ago, there was a boom in an allergy treatment offered through a company called Advanced Allergy Elimination. They promoted themselves heavily on television and in print media as being able to cure the most severe allergies.

Having moved to the country, I was sneezing a lot in spring and decided to try this therapy. The treatment involved holding a lot of small glass vials which contained the essence of different allergy groups such as wheat, dairy, pollens, dusts mites and so on. To test for an allergy, a handful of these vials are held in one hand, while the other arm is outstretched at shoulder height. The practitioner pushes on the outstretched arm and the patient tries to resist the arm being moved. If the arm goes down, it supposedly indicates that the substance caused weakness in the body and treatment is needed to heal this reaction. One allergy group can be treated as a time, ideally a week apart, costing several hundred dollars for each treatment. I tested sensitive to many substances.

To treat the allergy, an electric machine like a rough massage machine is run up and down the spine while the patient holds the vials. It was explained that it wasn't clear exactly how the treatment worked, but that by stimulating the meridians, the body somehow 'switched' from interpreting a substance that was irritating the body to interpreting it as harmless. For three days after a treatment for a supposed wheat allergy, I thought I felt a difference in the comfort and easy digestion of wheat products, but this didn't last. When I went back to the centre to ask if they could treat me again for the wheat allergy, the improvement I thought I had noticed on the first treatment was not experienced again.

In 2009, the Australian Competition and Consumer Commission investigated the company due to complaints from disgruntled customers who had lost thousands of dollars in the pursuit of a treatment for their allergies. The Commission found that the allergy company's claims were misleading and that the methods of the treatment were scientifically unverifiable. A court resolution was imposed on the company and it could no longer claim to identify, treat or cure allergies, essentially putting the company out of business.[26]

There are people who claim to have been healed through the Advanced Allergy Elimination treatments, including

Christians. For three days I thought that I was healed of sensitivity to wheat products. My explanation for this is that it is a counterfeit form of healing. The roots causes of some illnesses are spiritual and emotional, and demons can put allergy symptoms on people. I suggest that people who claim to have been healed through this New Age treatment actually have a spiritual root cause to their allergies and that a demon of infirmity or allergies simply shifted for a time or manifested some other symptom in the body. This is how the devil works: he allows a few people to believe they have been healed so that they become spokespeople who promote the treatment, thereby deceiving and confusing more people, leading them to open more doors to the demonic as well as losing a lot of time and money in pursuing bogus treatments.

Chiropractic

Although chiropractic isn't an outright New Age therapy, it is an alternative medicine practice that is still regarded with suspicion by mainstream medical practitioners. This may come as a surprise to many readers, as chiropractic medicine has established itself as a standard therapy for treating discomfort in the spine and joints. Many chiropractors do employ a number of techniques which are New Age or scientifically questionable and go against established medical understanding of how the anatomy works. Most medical texts note that chiropractic theory is not credible.

Chiropractic was founded in 1897 by Daniel Palmer who was a spiritualist and used magnets for healing, another dubious therapy. Palmer believed that all illness could be related back to misalignments in the spine, which he called 'subluxations.' He claimed that subluxations interrupted or impinged upon nerve impulses which affected the health of the body. Palmer believed in a divine 'life-force' energy that existed in the body and was affected by a misalignment. This claim has never been proven, and studies at Yale University demonstrated that misalignments do not function in the way chiropractic claims. In the study, chiropractors looking at the same sets of X-rays and patients were not able to find the same misalignments or agree on the specific condition that needed treatment.[27]

There are chiropractic practitioners today who still follow Palmer's teachings, and these are frowned upon by the medical community. More modern chiropractic schools follow scientific training similar to that undertaken by physiotherapists. Confusion is therefore created about the diverse and contradictory range of treatments available under the chiropractic umbrella.

Because chiropractors call themselves doctors, it is widely assumed by the general public that they train in a similar way to medical doctors. This is not the case. The concern with chiropractic is that so many practitioners utilise many New Age therapies such as 'applied kinesiology' or 'muscle testing' as it's also known, and other modalities such as iridology, homeopathy, reflexology and polarity therapy. Indeed, it was chiropractors who invented muscles testing and iridology, as well as The Reconnection I discussed earlier, and Body Electronics which I will discuss shortly. Many chiropractors claim to be able to treat conditions such as high blood pressure, psychological problems, diabetes, asthma and allergies, for example, which have no connection to musculoskeletal problems. Chiropractors who claim to be able to treat these conditions should be avoided as this would be a clear indication that they are mixing New Age practices with their treatments.

In the past, I have visited at least five different chiropractors for minor aches and pains caused from the stress of leaning over and correcting student essays for hours when I was a teacher. All of the chiropractors I visited used muscle testing and other New Age therapies and claimed to be able to help heal many illnesses, as listed above. Some people feel that they get a release of pain when they go to a chiropractor for a massage or spinal manipulation, but it invariably is only for a short time, and they must return regularly to regain the temporary relief. A physiotherapist explained to me that any change brought on by massage, stretching, manipulation or heat, for example, will have a short term effect on how you feel, but unless the underlying problem is dealt with, such as an imbalance in muscle strength or poor posture, then the problem will soon return. This is invariably the case with chiropractic. People are often encouraged to come in once or twice a week for a treatment, over a period of years. This is financial bondage! I asked one chiropractor about these long term treatment plans and he said that people could speed up their healing if they did simple exercises and stretching; however, because studies showed that most people were too lazy to do these exercises and preferred to come in and pay for a treatment, most chiropractors don't even bother suggesting exercise.

My recommendation to anyone who is considering seeing a chiropractor, is to go to a physiotherapist instead. Physiotherapists' understanding of the body is in line with accepted scientific knowledge of the anatomy; their training is more standardised than training for chiropractors; plus, they aim to correct and strengthen the weaknesses in the body by encouraging patients to do simple exercises.

Osteopathy

Occasionally I am also asked about osteopathy, which isn't as widely practised in Australia as chiropractic. The background of osteopathy is very similar to chiropractic and so the concerns with it are the same as for chiropractic treatment.

Bruno Gröning and the Circle of Friends

There's an important lesson to learn in this section of my testimony for people who call themselves Christians but don't go to church or fellowship with Christians who know the Bible very well. Being in this position makes you vulnerable to being deceived by things which might appear to be of God, like New Age healing, but are not. If you don't know the Bible intimately or have anyone spiritually sound to ask for advice, it's difficult to 'test the spirits to see whether they are from God, because many false prophets have gone out into the world.' (1 John 4:1) There are many forms of healing on offer that mix teaching or reference to Jesus Christ and the Bible with New Age concepts of God. I veered onto this path in the early months of my salvation for a very short time. While it's embarrassing to mention what I gullibly fell into, I feel it's important to make people aware of the range of traps and nonsense out there.

I forget how I found out about this group called 'Circle of Friends', but I went along to an information night to hear what they had to say about healing. There are only a very small number of people in Australia who are part of this group, most of them German. They follow the teaching of a man named Bruno Gröning, who was a German whose ministry in the 1950s saw extraordinary healings. Gröning professed Jesus Christ and wore a crucifix and so I thought that, 'By their fruit you will recognize them.' (Matthew 7:16) There were many documented testimonies of healing from this man who caused a great stir in Germany in the 1950s, so I assumed he was 'good fruit'. Being too curious for my own good, I decided to go along to watch a three hour documentary about Bruno Gröning's life and the miracles he saw. It was an interesting film and there were enough references to Jesus and the Bible and even a couple of Catholic priests approved him, so I thought there was no problem in turning up to one of this group's meetings.

The following week, I attended a meeting in Melbourne where a small group of about a dozen people sat in a room, facing a black and white picture of Bruno Gröning, sitting in the way Bruno had prescribed when he was alive: 'Bruno Gröning taught that the person should not cross arms and legs, when absorbing the divine energy, because this hinders the penetration of the healing stream. The hands should be laid like open flower cups on the thighs.'[28] The leader of the group started the meeting by calling on the presence of Bruno, Gröning: 'Bruno, are you with us?' I was surprised by this as it didn't seem right or Biblical and was very much like a séance in calling the spirits of the dead to answer. It wasn't what I saw Groening doing in the film when he prayed for people. I felt a disturbing heaviness on my chest and a slight jolt in my body. I didn't like this experience and didn't know what to make of it. The people in the group agreed that Bruno's presence seemed very strong that night. It was clear that these people looked to Bruno as a God-like figure. They believed that in praying to Bruno, they would be connected with God.

For a time I was confused because of the scripture Matthew 7:16; I thought the fruit that Bruno Gröning was documented to have seen when he was alive, was good. My interest in this group lasted for only three weeks. One day, as I was reading a Christian book, I read that we should never take one scripture in isolation, but in balance with other scriptures. It was then that I realised that one crucial scripture and aspect was missing in this type of healing offered by Bruno Gröning and his posthumous Circle of Friends: they weren't praying in Jesus' name or looking to Jesus, 'For there is one God and one mediator between God and mankind, the man Christ Jesus.' (1 Timothy 2:5) Although Gröning often quoted Jesus and referred to Him, he, 'never stated that only the Christian path leads to God. On the contrary, he clarified: "It makes absolutely no difference how the person finds God, the main thing is, that he finds God!"' [29]

I now know that:

If a prophet, or one who foretells by dreams, appears among you and announces to you a miraculous sign or wonder, and if the sign or wonder of which he has spoken takes place, and he says, 'Let us follow other gods' (gods you have not known) 'and let us worship them,' you must not listen to the words of that prophet or dreamer. The Lord your God is testing you to find out whether you love him with all your heart and with all your soul. (Deuteronomy 13:1-3)

Body Electronics

Body Electronics is a little-known form of New Age healing which will soon disappear altogether because its founder, US chiropractor and nutritionist, Dr John Whitman Ray, died in 2001 and the handful of people in Australia and America who follow his teachings disagree on key points. Further, they have little unity, time or motivation to promote, apply or develop his ideas.

I don't recall how I came across Body Electronics, but it was something I stumbled upon in the early months of becoming a Christian. The practice is largely based on eating a healthy, 70% raw diet and taking mineral supplements, in the belief that, given the right nutrition, the body can heal itself of any illness and regenerate itself. As there is a lot of common sense truth in this, at first I didn't see any concern in it.

Given that I had emerged from an extended period of extreme panic, anxiety, stress and fatigue, I was concerned about the damage to my adrenal and digestive systems and I was looking to cleanse and nourish my body to help it recover as quickly as possible.

Another aspect that first made me think that Body Electronics was a safe thing for me to explore as a Christian was that Dr Ray often quoted biblical scripture. He was a Mormon, and as I was only a new Christian, I didn't know much then about cultish forms of Christianity.

In addition to eating a healthy diet, people who follow Body Electronic look to get together in small groups to practise 'point holding,' a practice which involves applying pressure or 'pushing where the pain is' for typically 2-4 hours non-stop, to burn up calcium deposits or 'crystals' which they believe can hold sickness, negative experiences and pain in the body.

I went to an interstate retreat for a week to practise point holding and learn more about Body Electronics. Many Christians were amongst the group I was with, so my guard was again down in thinking there was no spiritual concern with it. However, in reading some on Dr Ray's teachings – which at first might seem like profound spiritual teachings that are challenging to grasp – I soon realised they are actually poorly written esoteric gobbledegook, typical of the New Age! For example: 'Until man can experience on the mental level, that which exists on the physical, he will be bound by the physical.'[30] As I struggled through reading parts of Dr Ray's books, a little concern crept in as I discovered that he freely quoted Buddha and other non-Christian teachers, along with Bible scriptures – another common deceit and confusion of the New Age.

Point holding is a lot like acupressure, but it involves holding for a much longer period of time. Some practitioners use iridology and sclerology (reading marks in the eyes) to determine the main health concerns and which areas of the body to attend to first. Dr Ray did develop his own chart of places on the body for point holding, but he also taught to 'push where the pain is' and some practitioners use acupuncture meridian points.

I had been told lots of wild stories of healings and strange reactions people experienced during point holding, but in the week that I participated in the point holding, I didn't witness or experience any noticeable healing among the group of twenty I was with, apart from people crying out in pain while they adjusted to having someone push hard, for 3-4 hours, non-stop, on a point - on the side of their groin, for example! And naturally, if you are the person holding a point, your pressing finger gets numb and hot from pushing on the one spot for hours.

Dr Ray referred to the burning or dissolving of the 'crystal' as the 'kundalini fire.' The kundalini is a Hindu spiritual concept, described as, 'an unconscious, instinctive…force… (that) lies coiled at the base of the spine. It is envisioned either as a goddess or else as a sleeping serpent...It is reported that kundalini awakening results in deep meditation, enlightenment and bliss. In practical terms, one of the most commonly reported kundalini experiences is the feeling of an electric current running along the spine.'[31]

Many in the New Age experience or aspire towards kundalini consciousness through yoga and meditation. It is interesting to note that it is common to find people at our healing meetings who come for prayer and deliverance and, as they are being prayed for, feel something they describe as being like a snake unravelling around their spine. My husband, John, has seen people writhe and slither on the floor like snakes, too.

Anyhow, it didn't take me long to realise that there were too many spiritual aspects to Body Electronics that did not measure up with what the Bible teaches is acceptable for a Christian to be involved with, so I repented of my involvement in it and walked away.

Other common New Age therapies that involve pseudo-science and quackery and have not stood up to scientific scrutiny.

- Blood type diet
- Homeopathy
- Craniosacral therapy
- Emotional Freedom Technique (EFT)
- Neuro Linguistic Programming (NLP)
- Magnet therapy
- Aromatherapy
- Herbal medicine
- Folk medicine
- Bach flower remedies
- Iridology
- Transcendental Meditation
- Crystal healing (A current pet hate of mine is the fad for amber necklaces for toddlers that are promoted as bringing relief to teething pain due to healing oils that are supposedly released from the amber).
- Animism (the belief that inanimate objects hold spiritual power)
- Aura reading
- Dowsing – spiritual divination through using a rod, pendulum or forked stick to locate water or information

If you would like to know more about the above therapies and others in the New Age, then I encourage you to invest in a copy of *Alternative Medicine: The Options, The Claims, The Evidence, How to Choose Wisely* by Donal O'Mathuna and Walt Larimore.[32]

Practices that require discernment to know what aspects are spiritually safe as they are often mingled with New Age concepts or therapies.

Naturopathy

Chiropractic

Osteopathic

Massage: there are many forms of massage which involve spiritual channelling of energy. Avoid the following: Reflexology; Kahuna massage (Hawaiian & Polynesian), Shiatsu, Thai Massage and virtually every form of Eastern massage.

Nutrition and dietetics

Beauty therapies

CONCLUSION

Jesus specialises in turning trials and tragedies into triumphs and my testimony is a classic example of this. What I thought was the worst thing that ever happened to me, turned out to be a blessing, because Jesus stepped into my situation when I was broken and without hope and He brought peace and restoration 'exceedingly abundantly above all that (I could) ask or think, according to the power that works in (me).' (Ephesians 3:20 WEB)

I found no healing through the New Age at all and lost thousands of dollars in the fruitless search. Through Jesus, I found healing - for free - for every area of my life: my physical body, my mind, my emotions, my wrong attitudes, my guilt and shame, my finances and my eternal spirit.

I now know the spirit world is very real and that there are two sides to this world: the kingdoms of light and darkness. Jesus heads the kingdom of light and His power and love are real and tangible and greater than anything the kingdom of darkness can offer. The New Age is one of many ways Satan uses to deceive people out of inheriting what Jesus died on the cross for: our eternal salvation, healing and forgiveness of sins. It is important for everyone to be aware of the spiritual forces behind New Age therapies, but most especially Christians who are seeking healing from Jesus. Involvement in the occult and New Age is a significant blockage to receiving healing because, 'You cannot drink the cup of the Lord and the cup of demons too.' (1 Corinthians 10:21)

Also, Christians need to be encouraged and reminded that atheists and people involved in the New Age, who may seem too hard or intimidating to approach, as I may have seemed, are in need of redemption and healing as much as anyone who is lost and broken. Braving their contempt to plant seeds of hope in pointing them towards Jesus is a challenge Christians must take up more purposefully. Few people would be offended by a gentle offer of prayer, for example. You see, *nothing* is more important than knowing Jesus and securing your eternal home in heaven.

Prayers

PRAYERS FOR SALVATION, FORGIVENESS AND HEALING

If there are parts of my testimony that have had an impact on you or shown you that there are areas in your life in which you might have opened doors to demonic spirits, then I encourage you to pray these following prayers out loud, and be specific in naming sins and people you need to forgive or release yourself from. For your prayers to have power and authority, it is important that you accept Jesus as Lord and open your heart to Him. If you have not opened your life to Jesus, then the first prayer listed is the most important, powerful, life-transforming prayer you could ever say. The Bible says that *'If you confess with your mouth that Jesus is Lord and believe in your heart that God raised him from the dead, you will be saved.'* (Romans 10:9)

Prayer to open your life to Jesus and have an eternal home in heaven

Lord Jesus, I open my heart to You and ask You to come into my life. I believe that You are the Son of God and that You died on the cross for my salvation, healing and forgiveness and that You rose again from the dead. Lord, I ask You to forgive all of my sins. I thank You, Jesus, for forgiving me, healing me and giving me an eternal home in heaven. I declare that You are my Lord, Jesus. Please guide me in every area of my life. Thank You for hearing my prayer. Amen.

I will sprinkle clean water on you, and you will be clean; I will cleanse you from all your impurities and from all your idols. I will give you a new heart and put a new spirit in you; I will remove from you your heart of stone and give you a heart of flesh. And I will put my Spirit in you and move you to follow my decrees and be careful to keep my laws. (Ezekiel 26:25-27)

Prayer to break sins of New Age/Occult involvement

Lord Jesus, I thank You that on the cross You took all my sin and suffering. I repent of all my contacts with Satan and his evil works. I renounce all involvement with witchcraft, the Occult and New Age. Specifically, I repent of being involved in (specifically name practices you've been involved in).........
...........................I repent and renounce all demon spirits that I have allowed to enter my life and I loose myself in the name of Jesus and command them to leave now, touching and harming no-one. Amen.

Prayer to repent of sins

Lord Jesus, I pray in Your name and I thank You that on the cross, You took all of my sins and suffering. I confess and renounce the following sins:

Pride, grumbling and complaining, fears, worry, stress, anxiety, anger, impatience, frustration, lack of self-control, self-pity, negative thoughts and words, ingratitude, lies, gossip, worldliness, judgmentalism, sexual immorality, lack of belief, jealousy and envy,.............(name any others). I ask You to forgive me, Jesus, and to wash me free from the consequences of these sins and deliver me from any demonic power that has affected me as a result of these sins. Jesus, help me to remain free of these sins and remind me to give my troubles over to You. Thank You, Jesus. Amen.

Breaking Soul Ties

Heavenly Father, I ask you to forgive me for any and all ungodly sexual relationships and soul ties, specifically with..........................(Be specific. Name each sexual partner.) In the name of the Lord Jesus Christ, I now renounce, break and loose myself from all demonic soul ties formed through sinful sexual encounters. Jesus, I ask that my spirit be loosed from them, and I tell my spirit to forget the unions and to be free from responsibility for them and emotional attachment to them. Lord, I choose to forgive each person that I have been involved with in any ungodly way. I choose to forgive myself and to no longer be angry, to hate or to punish myself. Lord, I thank you that you have totally cleansed and forgiven me, and that you love and accept me unconditionally. In the name of Jesus, I command all demons associated with perverse soul ties to go. Amen.

Prayer to forgive and deal with bitterness and resentment

Lord Jesus, I thank You that on the cross, You took all my sin and suffering. I come before You to repent of any unforgiveness, bitterness or resentment I've held towards people who have hurt me or who I've blamed for my problems, including myself and You, God. I choose to forgive........................... (name specifically) for having ....(be specific). I release these people to You, Lord. Please bless and heal them. And please release me, bless me and heal me and my emotions and memories. In Your name, Jesus, I command every evil spirit of unforgiveness to leave me now. Amen.

Prayer to break curses

Lord Jesus, I repent of every careless word that I have spoken intentionally or unwittingly over myself or others which has resulted in a curse. I ask that every curse that I've spoken be broken, and that freedom and blessings take its place. In the name of Jesus Christ I also confess all the sins of my forefathers, and by the redemptive blood of Jesus, I now break the power of every curse passed down to me through my ancestral line and from all demonic bondage placed upon us as the result of sins, transgressions or iniquities through myself, my parents or any of my ancestors. Christ has redeemed me from the curse of the law. I choose the blessing and reject the curse. In the name of my Lord Jesus Christ, I break the power of every evil curse spoken against me. I cancel the force of every prediction spoken about me, whether intentionally or carelessly, that was not according to God's promised blessings. I bless those who have cursed me. I forgive each person who has ever wronged me or spoken evil of me. In the name of Jesus, I command every evil spirit of curse to leave me now. Amen.

Prayer to break death wishes

Lord Jesus, I repent of and renounce all death wishes and the curse of premature death over my life. I declare that I shall not die, but live and declare the works of the Lord. In Your name, Jesus. Amen.

Prayer for people suffering anxiety and panic attacks

Lord Jesus, I come into Your presence and cast all my cares on you. Forgive me for carrying anxiety and worrying about things I can do nothing to change. Jesus, I ask that Your peace -which passes all understanding - fills me and stills my mind so that I am able to face my fears knowing that You are in control and going before me to make my path straight and to work all things together for the good of my life and my family. I thank You that You have not given me a spirit of fear but of power, love and a sound mind and I claim that for my life. Lord, I thank You that Your word says that You are my helper and very present in times of need.

When you pray these prayers, you should notice a new sense of release and peace come over you. If you feel that you still don't have freedom in a certain area, then find a church where there is a pastor or leader who is willing to pray though these prayers with you.

References and Endnotes

[1] Reconnective Healing: The Reconnection 2013, The Reconnection, Los Angeles, California, viewed throughout May 2012, < http://www.thereconnection.com/>.

[2] Quantum-Touch: The Power to Heal 2013, Quantum-Touch, Pismo Beach, California, viewed 11 May 2013, <http://www.quantumtouch.com/>.

[3] The Secret 2013, The Secret, viewed 11 May, 2013, <http://thesecret.tv/>.

[4] Leaf, C 2009, *Who Switched Off My Brain? Controlling Toxic Thoughts and Emotions*, Thomas Nelson Publishers, Southlake.

[5] Abraham-Hicks Publications 2013, Abraham-Hicks Publications, viewed 11 May 2013, <http://www.abraham-hicks.com/lawofattractionsource/about_abraham.php>.

[6] Ibid.

[7] Ibid.

[8] Theta Healing 2013, Nature Path, Inc. and the Theta Healing Institute of Knowledge, viewed throughout May 2012 and 11 May 2013, < http://www.thetahealing.com/>.

[9] Theta Magic 2009, this website link no longer exists, viewed in December 2010, <http://thetamagic.wordpress.com/2009/04/02/what-is-the-creator/>.

[10] Tricia Howell 2010, Theta Healing is a Fraud and a Dangerous Cult!, viewed 12 May, 2013, <http://fraudthetahealing.com/>.

[11] Reference Point Therapy, viewed throughout May 2012 and 12 May 2013, <http://www.referencepointtherapy.com/blog/>

[12] ThetaHealing – Unmasking the Cult, viewed throughout May 2012 and 11 May 2013, <http://www.thetahealing-un-masked.com/introduction.html>

[13] Ibid.

[14] Ibid.

[15] Prince, D 2007, *They Shall Expel Demons: What You Need to Know About Demons – Your Invisible Enemies,* Chosen Books
------ 2009, *Blessings or Curse You Can Choose: Freedom from Pressures You Thought You Had To Live With,* Chosen Books.

[16] DeGrandis, R 1996, *An Introduction to Inner Healing,* Praising God Catholic Association, Texas
Tapscott, B & DeGrandis, R 2005, Forgiveness and Inner Healing, Tyndale House Publishers, Illinois.

[17] Mansfield, S 2005, *Derek Prince's: A Biography*, Charisma House, Florida.

[18] John Mellor Ministries 2013, <www.johnmellor.org>.

[19] O'Mathuna, D & Larimore, W 2006, *Alternative Medicine: The Options, The Claims, The Evidence, How to Choose Wisely*, Zondervan, Michigan.

[20] British Parliamentary Commission into Alternative Medicine 1999- 2000, UK Parliament, viewed throughout May 2013, <http://www.parliament.the-stationery-office.co.uk/pa/ld199900/ldselect/ldsctech/123/12301.htm>

[21] Traditional Chinese Medicine Australia, viewed June 15, 2013, <http://www.tcmaustralia.com.au/>

[22] 'Deepak Chopra', *Wikipedia, The Free Encyclopedia,* viewed 11 May 2013, <http://en.wikipedia.org/wiki/Deepak_Chopra>.
**Normally I would avoid referencing Wikipedia, but as the

writer of the entry is accurate and articulately expresses my views about Chopra, it was worth quoting.

[23] Louise Hay.com, viewed June 20 2013, <http://www.louisehay.com/about-louise/>.

[24] 'Religious Science,' *Wikipedia, The Free Encyclopedia,* viewed 20 June 2013, <http://en.wikipedia.org/wiki/Religious_Science>.

[25] Australian College of Hypnotherapy, Sydney, NSW, viewed 20 June 2013, <http://www.careerinhypnosis.com.au/content_common/pg-eft.seo>.

[26] Australian Competition and Consumer Commission, viewed throughout May 2012, <http://www.accc.gov.au/media-release/accc-issues-contempt-proceedings-against-allergy-pathway-pty-ltd-and-paul-keir>.

[27] Palmer College of Chiropractic, The Palmer Family, viewed throughout May 2012, <http://www.palmer.edu/ThePalmerFamily/>.

[28] Bruno Gröning Circle of Friends 2013, viewed 11 May 2013, <http://www.bruno-groening.org/english/>.

[29] Ibid.

[30] Douglas W. Morrison: How We Heal, viewed throughout May 2013, <http://www.howweheal.com/>.

[31] Kundalini, Wikipedia, *The Free Encyclopedia, viewed 14 July 2013* http://en.wikipedia.org/wiki/Kundalini

[32] O'Mathuna, D & Larimore, W 2006, *Alternative Medicine: The Options, The Claims, The Evidence, How to Choose Wisely*, Zondervan, Michigan.